Eagle

Animal
Series editor: Jonathan Burt

Eagle

Janine Rogers

REAKTION BOOKS

For Bill and Brian, birders

Published by
REAKTION BOOKS LTD
33 Great Sutton Street
London EC1V 0DX, UK
www.reaktionbooks.co.uk

First published 2015
Copyright © Janine Rogers 2015

Printed and bound in China by C&C Printing Co. Ltd

A catalogue record for this book is available from the British Library

ISBN 978 1 78023 337 6

Contents

Introduction

A few years ago I sat with a friend on a beach on the Northumberland Strait, a narrow body of water that divides Prince Edward Island from Nova Scotia and New Brunswick, watching the birds take advantage of the low tide. A bald eagle flew into view; we admired its dramatic markings and powerful flight. It made a few passes over the flats, moving more slowly and deliberately than the other seabirds. Suddenly it became a dark streak and struck a black cormorant in mid-air with breathtaking speed and precision. The two birds fell to the sea floor, the cormorant (which is not a small bird) struggling desperately. On the ground the eagle looked twice the size it had in the air – it dragged its frantic prey behind a low rock and began to tear at it. Although the rock hid the worse of the violence, we were horrified at what followed. For long moments we could see the cormorant's head or wing wave over the rock as the victim thrashed: the eagle was eating it alive.

In those few minutes we had witnessed many of the associations people have with eagles. Across cultures and through millennia, eagles have been known for their elegance, power and cruelty, and these characteristics have caused eagles to be among the most mythologized and storied of birds. Human emotions towards eagles range from reverence to repugnance and yet they are also deeply mysterious to us. As a general rule,

A majestic bald eagle flies over its nest.

they tend to live on the fringes of the human world – they are rarely tamed – and, even in the case of the largest and most dramatic eagles like the golden eagle and the bald eagle, our imaginations about their lives often outstrip our actual knowledge because we are forced to observe them at a distance. And yet while our scientific understanding of eagles has been hard-won, eagles are far from unknown in the larger sense: being birds of such rough beauty and aggression, they are a conspicuous presence in many cultural narratives. Often called 'the king of the birds', eagles rule in the human imagination as much as they rule the ecosystems they inhabit.

Their place at the top of the food chain, however, presents an inborn vulnerability for these magnificent birds. Like many other major predators, they breed slowly; even in optimal conditions eagles just barely maintain their populations. Our modern world, of course, is forming ecologies that are far from optimal for eagles and many species are endangered by pollution, urban sprawl, habitat destruction and direct persecution by people. As a result, we are at risk of losing a key character in our ecological, cultural and perhaps even psychological landscapes.

Broadly speaking, the eagle is a symbol of paradox and liminality – states of contradiction and in-betweenness. Symbols like this can refer simultaneously to two oppositional things at once or to something that refuses absolute categories of understanding. Much of this symbolic ambiguity can be traced to the real lives of eagles and their function in the biological world. They are the *über*-hunter, often seen as the red tooth and claw of nature as they weed out the sick, the weak, the slow and the unlucky. They gorge themselves on the flesh of the innocent, and not only that, but on the decaying corpses of the already dead. They seem voracious and indiscriminate – a random killing machine, a thief and a scavenger who is lazy with the opportunistic cruelty

of the criminal. Even their infants kill – each other. On the positive side, we see eagles as noble: large, powerful, with the proverbially piercing eyes that seem to watch over us. They soar amazingly high and fast, with apparently little effort. They are long-lived, (mostly) loyal to their mates and attentive parents. They are clever and resourceful. They are beautiful. Religious beliefs are built around them.

In all of our imaginative ideas of eagles these polarities and contradictions persist. And indeed, in the realm of the gods eagles are the bringers of life and death equally. Fair-minded observers have long noticed that even the apparently disgusting behaviours of eagles have positive effects; carrion eaters clean the world of decayed corpses, bacteria and disease, creating a healthy environment so that others may live. We come full circle; the eagle is a resurrectionist. The eagles of Zeus communicate his often arbitrary and inscrutable wishes to men; capable of great vision, but also motiveless cruelty, the god and his familiars are perfectly matched. North American eagles carry us between the land of the living and the land of the dead – and it is not necessarily a one-way journey. As a bird of destruction and resurrection the eagle is extended into fantastical creatures like the phoenix, as well as hybrid beings like the gryphon and the sphinx. A figure of death, but also regeneration; a symbol of freedom, but also tyranny; we look to the eagle to exemplify the best and the worst qualities of our own existence, and of ourselves.

1 Eagles Themselves: Biology and Ecology

Would you know an eagle if you saw one? Most of us, even those of us who are not birdwatchers or biologists, think we have a rough idea of what eagles are, although our specific images might be quite different. If you live in North America as I do, you would almost certainly think first of the bald eagle. If you are British or Continental European, the golden eagle might spring to mind if you are in the north, or the imperial eagle if you are in the Mediterranean area. If you are Australian, the wedge-tailed eagle is probably your primary image; if you are South American, the harpy eagle. Readers from Africa or the Indian subcontinent may have the most varied concept of 'eagle'; there are many there to choose from. Wherever you are, and whatever your specific eagle impressions, you might be surprised to discover how broad and fluid the term 'eagle' actually is.

The word 'eagle' is not a scientific word; it does not refer to a single species or even a specific genus. Rather, it refers to a general category of raptors that possess certain attributes that together constitute a type of bird that is carnivorous, diurnal and often large in comparison to most other flighted birds. Colloquially speaking, many of us who live in Eurasia, Australia or North America probably have a fairly clear idea of what we mean by 'eagles': when asked to describe an eagle we probably refer to some common features. Size might be the first, for many eagles are big, often the biggest of the predatory birds in a given area. Indeed the standard definition of 'eagle' in the *Oxford English Dictionary* begins with size: 'large bird of prey of family Accipitridae, with keen vision and powerful flight'.

In fact, the word 'eagle' is an Anglicization of the French *aigle*, which comes from the Latin *aquila*, meaning dark or black. As the eminent ornithologist Leslie Brown points out, however, the idea that eagles are big, dark birds comes primarily from a European context – it is the sort of definition Aristotle used in describing eagles, for example – and the definition does not always apply to more southerly contexts, especially Africa and South America, where eagles like the harpy eagle are often grey or have significant amounts of white, red and tawny colours.[1] Furthermore, some species of eagles are actually quite small, especially the genus called 'snake-eagles' or 'serpent-eagles', as well as a group of birds designated 'hawk-eagles' that, as their name suggests, combine some characteristics of the two types of bird, including the smaller size of the hawks. The Great Nicobar serpent eagle is usually considered the smallest eagle and weighs only about a pound (the 'Great' is in reference to its island home, not the bird itself).

Other attributes that we may associate with 'eagles' are their hunting behaviour, their power in flight and their intimidating appearance. These general impressions connect to specific physical features: a vicious-looking beak; powerful, grasping claws; piercing eyes and so on. These broad strokes of identification are indeed useful in labelling eagles as a category to the non-specialist. But for biologists the word 'eagle' is a broad and somewhat loose descriptor that actually includes birds from a few different classifications.

In terms of most of the evolutionary story of eagles, they share a narrative with the majority of other birds on the planet.

The earliest reptiles of the Paleozoic era split into two lines, the synapsids from which came the mammals, and the diapsids from which came the crocodiles, lizards, snakes and birds. The diapsids led to the archosaurs and then the dinosaurs, which after a couple of more divisions produced the theropods and then the maniraptors. Some characteristics of eagles were becoming evident with the evolution of the latter. Even the name, maniraptor (or 'hand seizer', that which grabs with its hands or claws), provides a hint as to what this line will become, especially in regard to raptors like eagles, which do indeed seize their prey in their claws. While the evolutionary history of birds is still complex and contested, the maniraptors excite ornithologists because there is considerable evidence that they may have had feathers (including the venerable *T. rex* – at least at birth); this, however, is still speculative.[2] We do know, however, that some had feathers,

A white-tailed eagle in Svolvaer, Norway soars above the treeline.

although feathers do not necessarily mean flight in these cases. The maniraptors subdivided many times, eventually producing the Avialae class, which produced the (usually) flying, feathered animals that today we recognize as 'birds'. This included both the Jurassic *Archaeopteryx*, which is widely (and somewhat controversially) described as the earliest bird, although it is not a direct ancestor of modern birds.[3] The Avialae class also produced the neornithines, 'new birds', in the Cretaceous period (145–66 MYA), from which we get our modern birds. Subdividing further, we come to the Neoaves, and further still, to the order Falconiformes, which includes the eagles, hawks, falcons and vultures. Thus today's eagles are the result of millennia of evolution and diversification.

The classification of bird species is confusing. One of the first attempts to classify and account for animal life comes from Aristotle. Unfortunately Aristotle made some errors in his eagle classification, sometimes confusing eagles with other types of bird, especially vultures and falcons. He also had only limited information drawn from direct observation and came to some dodgy conclusions regarding the habits and life cycles of birds, including eagles. For centuries other writers on ornithology, such as Pliny the Elder and Aelian of Praeneste, perpetuated Aristotle's mistakes. In the Middle Ages Aristotle's ideas were mixed in with folkloric and theological interpretations of animals in medieval bestiaries (books of beasts), a popular form that descended from the *Physiologus*, an ancient bestiary compiled in Alexandria. In the thirteenth century the Hohenstaufen Emperor Frederick II noted the weaknesses in Aristotle's ornithology and aimed to correct some of these misconceptions in *The Art of Falconry*, based on his own experience with raptors in falconry, although very little of his book deals with eagles.[4] Nevertheless, some of Aristotle's misapprehensions regarding birds persisted into the twentieth

A fossil of the eagle's prehistoric ancestor, the *Archaeopteryx*, in the Museum für Naturkunde, Berlin.

century.[5] Even today, however, there are problems categorizing certain eagle types and their relationship to other birds.

Today the problem with classifying eagles is that, as in virtually all other fields of taxonomy, different systems of classification are used by different researchers. Field ornithologists tend to use morphological systems that categorize the birds according to their physical and behavioural attributes, while evolutionary biologists use biochemical methods to classify birds according to their evolutionary relationships. According to current classification, all eagles belong to the biological order Falconiformes, which includes all the diurnal raptors: vultures, hawks, falcons and osprey. The largest family of the Falconiformes order is the Accipitridae, which includes 237 species, about 75 of which are eagles, grouped into about 21 genera. Recently DNA research has resulted in significant reclassifications of eagle genera; most notably, the group of eagles once in the *Hieraaetus* genus have been moved to the *Aquila* genus, and two *Aquila* eagles – the greater and lesser spotted eagles – have been moved to the *Lophaetus* genus.[6] Some of the suggested changes are contentious and at the time of writing are still under discussion; there are almost certainly other changes to come. Because the classifications keep shifting, it might be helpful to group eagles according to five categories determined by broad characteristics: booted or 'true' eagles, sea or fish eagles, snake or serpent eagles, hawk-eagles and large tropical forest eagles.

The booted or 'true' eagles include such high-profile species as the golden eagle, wedge-tailed eagle and Spanish imperial eagle. These are called booted eagles because they have feathers on their tarsi, which are the shanks of the legs that are usually featherless. Note, though, that there is also a species in the *Aquila* genus called in English the 'Booted Eagle', so all Booted Eagles are booted eagles, but not all booted eagles are Booted Eagles. Confused? Welcome to the wacky world of bird classification:

A falconer holding a Steller's sea eagle in the Yorkshire Dales, England.

this is why ornithologists prefer to used scientific species terms; the Booted Eagle species name is *Aquila pennata* . . . but it used to be *Hieraaetus pennata*. The original *Aquila* eagles tended to be large, although the addition of the *Hieraaetus* genus to the *Aquila* genus has added more modest-sized birds to this group.

The second category of eagles consists of the sea eagles, including the bald eagle and the white-tailed eagle, as well as the impressive Steller's sea eagle, which is one of the largest eagles. Sea eagles are actually genetically closer to kites than other eagle types, but of course they are commonly recognized as eagles. The third category, snake or serpent eagles, are also not considered 'true' eagles in the strictest genetic classification.[7] These smaller eagles, which, as their name suggests, eat snakes and other small reptiles, are found mostly in Africa and Indomalayan regions, although the short-toed snake eagle is also found in parts of Europe. Very little is known about some of the serpent eagles, including the mysterious Nias and Semeulue serpent eagles, which are hardly ever seen and have rarely been studied.

The fourth category – the hawk-eagles – is made up of tropical forest birds that often have crested feathers on their head. There are thirteen species of hawk-eagle in the forests of the Indomalaya ecozone and Central and South America. The ambiguity of their name reflects the overlap possible with other raptor categories. In the tropical forests we also find the eagle category with the fewest members: the four large tropical eagles, consisting of the massive harpy eagle and Philippine eagle, as well as the crested eagle and the New Guinea harpy eagle. These four eagles are grouped together because they fill a similar ecological niche, eating monkeys, sloths and other large mammals of the forest. Their ecological similarities may be an example of convergent evolution, as not all four seem to be closely connected in DNA studies. Convergent evolution is when two distinct evolutionary lines develop similar ecological functions and therefore similar body forms; so two birds, like the Philippine eagle and harpy eagle, might

Taxidermied Philippine eagle at Ninoy Aquino Parks and Wildlife Center.

look very similar and behave in similar ways, but actually not come
from the same evolutionary line. In fact, the Philippine eagle has
recently been found to be genetically closer to snake eagles.[8] Many
still group the Philippine eagle with the harpy eagle because of
its size and eating habits, but its genetic affiliations are important
as well and thus it can be said to have a foot in both categories. To
make matters even more confusing, these four eagles are sometimes called 'harpy eagles' as a group (as distinct from the harpy
eagle species, *Harpia harpyja*).

Finally there are some species of eagle that don't appear to fit
neatly into any of the five major groups: the black-chested buzzard

eagle, the martial eagle, the African crowned eagle, the Indian black eagle and the long-crested eagle are all distinct from each other and other eagle species, while the crowned and black solitary eagles are related only to each other. Further genetic research may determine the nature of the relationships between these 'miscellaneous' eagles and other kinds of eagles.

Many eagle species have subspecies, although these levels of classification are also contested. Still, some ornithologists distinguish between northern and southern bald eagles, for example, or six subspecies of golden eagle. Subspecies are often determined by subtle differences found among species that cover very large territories. The six subspecies of the golden eagle give an indication of its immense range: *Aquila chrysaetos chrysaetos* (northwest Europe, including Britain), *A. c. homeyeri* (North Africa, Iberian peninsula and Middle East), *A. c. daphanea* (Himalayas), *A. c. kamtschatica* (Siberia), *A. c. canadensis* (North America) and *A. c. japonica* (Japan and Korea).[9] Eagles are also sometimes grouped into superspecies, wherein multiple closely related species inhabit the same ecological niche in different but connected areas: for example, several large *Aquila* eagles – golden eagle, Verreaux's eagle, wedge-tailed eagle and Gurney's eagle – replace each other as we move around the globe until we get to South America, where this superspecies group is not represented (large eagles are represented in South America by the harpy eagle).[10]

The eagles we have today do not constitute all the eagles that have ever existed on earth. There are eagle species that went extinct centuries ago; Haast's eagle is a fascinating example of this. Haast's eagle (named after Julian Haast, who found the first skeleton in 1871) lived in New Zealand, apparently until the fifteenth or sixteenth century. It had a wingspan of nine feet or more, and weighed almost 30 lb (14 kg). It is speculated that it fed mostly on moas, ostrich-like birds that are now also extinct. The moas were bigger than modern ostriches, so the fact that Haast's eagle was able to kill them (hitting them from the side and taking them down that way) is even more impressive. Unfortunately the extinction of Haast's eagle was almost certainly caused by the arrival of humans in New Zealand, who competed with the great birds for food sources, especially the moas, which were hunted to extinction. Other eagle species became extinct on the islands of Hawaii and in North America as people arrived in previously unpopulated areas. As is the case today, human-caused extinctions of eagles were more likely to be the result of habitat destruction than hunting the birds directly.[11]

Today eagles exist on every continent except Antarctica. Some species are highly localized and are found only in a very small area, such as individual islands like Madagascar. Other species are much more broad-ranging, especially the golden eagle, as mentioned above, which is the species that covers the largest global area since much of the northern hemisphere is home to one of its six subspecies. Most eagle species live in Eurasia and Africa. Only the bald eagle and the golden eagle can be found in North America; in Central and South America we find several eagle species.

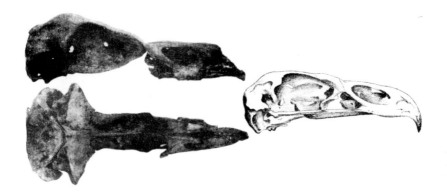

Images of a Haast's eagle (*Harpagornis moorei*) skull from *Transactions and Proceedings of the Royal Society of New Zealand* (1893).

Aquila gurneyi, or
Gurney's eagle.

Eagle terrain varies with the species – from deep forests to open savannah to rocky shorelines – and the environments for specific eagle species determine their diets (and vice versa, as species have adapted specific environmental requirements based on their food preferences). Obviously, fish-eating eagles require bodies of water where fish are close enough to the surface to catch, and monkey-eating eagles require the heavy forests of their prey's habitat. Some species can switch terrain according to their life cycles; the greater spotted eagle, which is one of the eagle species that migrates long distances, lives in forested areas in Eurasia for part of the year and open savannah in Africa for the rest.[12] Although

The ancient Giant Haast's eagle is an extinct species of eagle that once lived in the South Island of New Zealand. It is depicted here attacking its prey, the New Zealand moa.

eagles with large ranges like the golden eagle must of necessity adapt to different climates and ecosystems, there are often common qualities to even the most diverse of territories; specifically, golden eagle habitat tends to have a lot of open space with excellent sightlines. Golden eagles are very adaptable and can even live in both arctic and desert regions. Their ideal landscape, however, seems to be mountainous regions with a mix of wooded areas and open fields.[13]

As we have seen, many of us associate eagles with size: the best-known species in the West tend to be larger than most other birds, excepting vultures and very large geese and swans. That said, the size of eagles as a bird type varies from a little over 1 lb (in the Great Nicobar serpent eagle) to around 20 lb (in the harpy and Steller's sea eagles).[14] In most species the female is larger than the male; this is typical of raptors and some speculate that this is because the males need to be more agile as hunters.[15] This characteristic is called 'reversed sexual dimorphism' ('reversed' because in most mammals, including humans, the average male is larger than the female; we tend to use our own biology as the norm).[16]

The impressive size of many eagle species is not just a matter of weight, but also wingspan. The eagles with the largest wingspan include the golden eagle: the females in the Himalayan and Siberian subspecies have wings spanning over eight feet. In some cases, however, eagles are not quite as big as human imaginations would have them; 'most people', notes Penny Olsen, speaking of the Australian wedge-tailed eagle, 'are disappointed, when the tape measure comes out, to learn that the eagle is somewhat smaller than an F-111 and weighs less than the average house cat'.[17] Eagle dimensions are adapted to specific environments. For example, eagles that live in forests tend to have shorter wings proportional to their bodies than those that live in more open environments, to facilitate flight through trees and undergrowth; the harpy eagle, the Philippine eagle and the extinct Haast's eagle are all examples of this, for although they are the largest eagles by weight, they do not have the greatest wingspans.

Visually, even the smaller eagle species present an intimidating appearance; they tend to have larger-looking heads and beaks than other birds of prey, and they are often more powerful or heftier in comparison to the lighter-boned hawks. Despite the impressive head, the most dangerous part of the eagle is its feet. In fact, the order name 'Falconiformes' derives from the Latin word *falx* (genitive *falcis*), which means 'sickle', obviously inspired by the curved talons that eagles and other raptors in the order use to kill their prey. The eagle's hunting method is usually to grab its prey at high speed, relying in large part on the force of the blow and the strength of the grip to kill or at least stun the victim. The birds can grab their prey because three of their talons face forwards and one faces backwards, contracting together into a grip that is estimated in large eagles at about 200 lb per square inch (or 14 kg/cm^2). After grasping its prey, the eagle's talons contract powerfully, aided by a 'ratchet-like system' of muscles in the legs and toes.[18] The late raptor expert Leslie Brown reported that the grip of a large eagle is 'suffocating' and 'must be experienced to be believed' (although obviously he wasn't recommending it).[19] The grip drives the hind talon into the prey like a dagger and Brown speculated that eagles can be very precise in finding the 'vital spot', even with very large or struggling prey. There are several stories of well-intentioned eagle researchers being pierced straight through the hand or arm (even while wearing protective gloves) by the talon of a panicky eagle. The claws of eagles each have special adaptations for their specific hunting requirements. Eagles that eat monkeys, like the Philippine eagle for example, have different claws from fish eagles like the bald eagle, whose feet have scaled

surfaces that assist them in picking up slippery prey.[20] The larger eagles that hunt bigger types of prey have tarsi with muscle (where most birds just have bone and tendons) to assist them in gripping and lifting their dinner. Eagles that hunt snakes have thick scales on their tarsi to protect them from venomous bites.

Although their impressive beaks are meant for tearing flesh, eagles do not usually use their beaks to deliver the coup de grâce, unlike falcons. Rather, the beak's purpose is primarily for eating. In fact, eagles are not overly concerned with waiting until their prey is dead; since their beaks are not adapted for killing, if the initial blow does not kill the prey, eagles may have little choice but to go forward with consuming the animal, which surely reinforces their reputation for cruelty. Beaks grow continuously, and are worn down by eating and rubbing the upper and lower parts together.

One of Aristotle's misconceptions regarding eagles was the idea that when the birds grew old the beak stopped wearing away until the upper mandible obstructed the mouth and the bird died of hunger. Although this is not the case, some birds in captivity should have their beaks trimmed if they don't wear naturally.[21]

The call of an eagle varies with the species, but in general the eagle has never been praised for its melodic voice (but then none of the raptors are renowned for their musicality). In popular culture the eagle's scream often signifies its fierceness, and though many species do have a scream in their repertoire, the more common voices of eagles seem to be unimpressive. One expert remarked that the voice of the bald eagle is 'ridiculously weak and insignificant, more of a squeal than a scream, quite unbecoming a bird of its size and strength'. Another compared its voice to an 'unoiled castor'.[22] Some filmmakers are reputed to overdub the bald eagle's voice with the more impressive voices of other birds, like the red-tailed hawk.[23] Other eagle species make a range of sounds, including barking or quacking. Penny Olsen reports that the Australian wedge-tailed eagle's vocalizations can include a

A close-up shot of a beautiful and powerful golden eagle in Wisentgehege Springe Game Park, Hanover, Germany.

'rather sweet' range of sounds.[24] The 'powerful, piercing' cry of the African fish eagle has been called the 'call that symbolizes Africa'.[25] Many eagles, however, tend to be fairly quiet, at least when humans are present.

One part of eagle anatomy that fascinates people is the eye; indeed, 'eagle-eyed' is a metaphor and a bit of cliché, but it does refer to a specific reality of eagles: they do indeed have exceptionally powerful vision. Experts gauge that their vision is up to two and a half or three times that of human vision (some say higher), but this rough estimate does not really convey a true description of eagle sight. It is not simply that they can see further than we do: they see the world in a fundamentally different manner. Eagles can see movement much more quickly, and from further away, than we do. They can see 'faster' than humans, if you will. Because they have more receptor cells in the retina, they can process details more quickly, focusing swiftly on objects at greater distances than we can see. All birds can also see light differently than us; they can see near ultraviolet light that we cannot, and they can perceive higher contrasts of colour – especially blues and greens – which is an important ability in their celestial and verdant worlds.[26] It has been hypothesized that eagles might be able to see scent trails that some mammals leave, and they may be capable of infrared vision, in which case they would actually be able to see the thermal air currents they so love to ride.[27] Eagles, like all birds, can't move their eyes in their skulls very much, so they have to move their entire heads in order to change their direction of vision. But eagles and other raptors have an advantage over most other birds (which often make up their prey) in that their more forward-facing eyes give them binocular vision as well as monocular vision. Binocular vision allows them to have depth perception – clearly a critical feature for zeroing in on prey from a distance, then striking at full fatal force.

Eagle eyes are huge, proportionally much bigger in their faces than our eyes are in our faces (their eyes are actually about the same size as ours in direct comparison). We can only see a bit of the eye when we look at an eagle – most of it is deep in the skull. The cornea, which is only a fraction of the eye, bulges out slightly to fit into the front of the eye socket. The eagle's distinctive patrician brow, which often defines its anthropomorphic representation as old, wise, judgemental or regal, is technically called a 'supraorbital ridge'. This bony ridge cuts the glare of the sun high up in the air and shields the eye somewhat from branches and other objects when flying through forests. Eagle eyes are also protected by a nictitating membrane, which is a second lid under the exterior eyelid that draws across the eye horizontally to block potential injury. This membrane also moistens the eye in flight. Eagle eyes are usually yellow or brown, and they change colour with the different stages of the bird's life; juveniles often have darker eyes than adults. There has been some speculation regarding the connection between eye colour and eye function: it has been noted that certain types of eagle (snake-eaters, for example) tend to have a specific eye colour (yellow, in that example), but it is difficult to draw absolute conclusions.[28] Many other eagles also have yellow eyes; the striking yellow eyes in the white head of the bald eagle lend much to its fierce beauty.

Because eagles are diurnal hunters, vision is their most important sense, but hearing can also be important in hunting. The huge harpy eagle of South America has a distinctive facial disc that may amplify its hearing; this is useful for hunting in dense forests where the line of sight is limited. Eagles, like many other birds, do not seem to have highly developed senses of smell or taste, although they can probably smell fresh carrion and have been known to reject food that is too far gone.

With the wide range of eagle species comes a wide range of eating habits, although all eagles are carnivores. Eagle dietary

Circaetus fasciolatus, or southern banded snake eagle.

preferences have named and categorized many of them: snake eagles and fish eagles, most obviously. But most eagles have more varied diets than their names might suggest. The bald eagle, which is a fish eagle, specializes in salmon, but also eats small mammals and other birds. Most eagles are carrion eaters as well as hunters of fresh food; they will help themselves to the kills of other animals, as well as abandoned dead animals and roadkill. In fact, bald eagles seem to prefer dead fish lying on the banks over live fish in the water. Some observers characterize this as their laziness, but it is more likely that given the high rate of hunting failure in raptors, carrion is a safer bet in terms of the energy output versus nutritional input. Many eagles prefer to hunt earlier in the day, although opportunity must be seized when it presents itself and often they have to adapt to the habits of their prey. Once they have fed, large eagles spend much of the day at rest, perching and loafing. Eagles can eat large amounts of food at one go, storing it in their crop, then digesting it for some hours. After large meals it may not be necessary for them to eat again for some days.[29] Some species will cache prey – hiding unfinished kills in a safe spot to eat later.[30]

Eagles hold the record of all birds for greatest weight-carrying capacity. Apparently the winning entry in the United States was a bald eagle lifting a 15 lb (6.8 kg) mule deer;[31] there is no note as to how far the bird got with the deer. One is inclined to think not very far, since the average bald eagle itself weighs 9 lb (male) to 13 lb (female). Eagles can kill animals much larger than they can carry; when they do, they must either consume the dead animal where they kill it (if on the ground, this might leave the eagle vulnerable to attack itself) or leave much of the carcass behind. Therefore, killing prey too big to carry involves some risk and it is not something that eagles do very frequently. When they do, however, these kills have some virtue in a larger ecological sense since a large kill can provide food for other scavengers. Both

An eagle seizing a fox that was approaching its nest, illustrated in *Die Gartenlaube* in 1887.

avian and mammal scavengers also benefit from the ability of eagles to easily open up a carcass with their powerful beaks.

Because eagles are raptors that by definition grab with their claws, they require certain techniques and circumstances for a successful kill. The fish eaters, for example, cannot dive into the water so they are dependent on grabbing fish close to the surface. This limits them to certain types of fish at certain times of the year, such as salmon, which are close to the surface when moving upstream to spawn in shallower waters. Some eagles also eat crabs and turtles, breaking them open by dropping them onto rocks (the playwright Aeschylus was said to have been killed by an eagle dropping a tortoise on him; this story is likely apocryphal, but theoretically it is possible).[32] Many eagles hunt other birds in flight; smaller eagles like the Booted Eagles and Ayres's hawk-eagles

make aerial hunting a speciality. Eagles also hunt from perches, simply dropping down on their prey as it appears beneath them; the African crowned eagle hunts small forest antelopes in this manner.[33] It is not uncommon to see eagle pairs, especially *Aquila* eagles, hunting cooperatively: working together, they can take down much larger prey than themselves.

Harpy eagle caught mid-flight in the Camino del Oleoducto, Parque Nacionale Soberania, Panama, December 2006.

Snake and serpent eagles have smaller, thicker toes for gripping snakes and other slender reptilian prey, and once they land on a snake they can usually break its back very quickly. Some species will even take on very large or poisonous snakes, although this kind of hunting is obviously risky. White-bellied sea eagles favour sea snakes, which are highly poisonous, and it appears that the grey-headed fishing eagle in Cambodia prefers water snakes to fish.[34] A snake could of course strike an eagle that made a clumsy attack, although this is apparently rare. The eagles seem to be able to digest snake venom through the stomach, although they are not immune to a bite. If the snake is very large, it might be consumed in parts, but usually smaller snakes are consumed whole, headfirst.[35]

Piracy is a key survival strategy for all types of eagle, especially fish eagles; they will steal from other birds and other predators as well as from each other. Although often perceived as ignoble, piracy, especially when it occurs between eagles, has the added benefit of spreading the nutritional wealth more evenly among an eagle population.[36] When stealing from other eagles, pirates are likely able to judge how much resistance they will meet by the bulge in the other bird's crop: if the other bird appears to have eaten a good amount it is less likely to put up a serious fight.[37] Sea eagles will obtain their fish by stealing it from more effective fishing birds like ospreys as a way of conserving energy in the process of finding food. They will also steal from human hunters, taking away small trapped animals like muskrats – the carcass, trap and all.[38]

When an eagle hunts an animal outside its usual purview, especially when it attacks something much larger than itself or something that is a 'high-risk' prey (such as a domestic animal in close proximity to people), it may be due to 'hunger panic' caused by extreme hunger or near starvation. Without the right hunting and feeding requirements in place, eagles are vulnerable; in February 2011, for example, a poor salmon run in British Columbia, Canada, caused famine among the bald eagle population. There were reports of eagles falling out of trees from starvation, as well as simply falling from the sky to drown in the ocean and rivers, or hitting roofs and other objects. The desperate birds turned to rubbish dumps for both food and the heat given off from the rotting refuse (the loss of body fat, and therefore warmth, was as dangerous as the lack of nutrition). But with this choice there were new hazards; eating poisoned vermin carcasses that had been thrown out with the household rubbish killed several birds.[39]

'Fly like an eagle' is another cliché but, like many clichés, it exists for a reason. Eagles are powerful fliers; their wings are larger proportionally to their bodies than those of other birds, and as with many other raptors, the wingtips are 'slotted', which gives the wings their distinctive 'fingered' look. These wings give eagles stability while in flight, as they can adjust the primary feathers at their wingtips in order to offset wind turbulence; this stability is obviously helpful in hunting, as the birds can focus more clearly on their prey.[40] The speeds of eagles' flights and the heights they can reach are truly impressive. The normal migrating speed of the golden eagle is 28 to 32 miles per hour (44–50 km/h), which is notable although other raptors, especially hawks, are known to be faster. In dives, eagles can be astoundingly fast – up to 120 miles per hour (190 km/h) for a golden eagle.[41] The speed of the descent, coupled with the weight of an eagle's body, is what often produces the killing strike force in its attack on prey.

The impressive height of eagle flight is usually produced by thermal soaring, where they ride pockets of warm air rising up from the earth. In mountain ranges, winds that strike mountains are diverted upwards and these updrafts provide soaring opportunities; eagles and other raptors take advantage of these lifts, particularly during migration. Soaring is an important aspect of the imaginative associations that many cultures have with eagles. They are often associated with the sun, which may be an unconscious observation of the fact that soaring activities occur when there is sun warming the air and causing it to rise upward, creating a current on which the birds can soar. Without good soaring conditions, eagles often stay close to the ground; they tend not to fly in rain, either, unless they live in very wet climates like that in Scotland, where presumably they have become inured to the damp.[42]

Many eagles do hunt while soaring, but surveying their territory and staying cool are also reasons for this behaviour.[43] Some soaring seems to be recreational; eagles soar because they can. One of the most spectacular types of eagle flight is the courtship behaviour of aerial gymnastics; eagle pairs may soar and dive together, sometimes engaging in mock combat. Golden eagles and wedge-tailed eagles perform high spirals, then take plunging

Bruno Liljefors,
Sea Eagle's Nest,
1907, oil on canvas.

dives towards the ground; the bald eagle dips and spins like an airborne dancer, sometimes linking talons with its partner (this is called 'talon grappling') – the imperial eagle is also famous for this kind of display. These flight displays are integral to the social and familial structure of eagle life.

Most eagle species are assumed to be largely monogamous, in the sense that they tend to have only one mate at a time and usually continue the relationship until the death of one of the pair, but it has been pointed out that this is difficult to prove definitively. Nevertheless, even if monogamy is the norm, there have been recorded cases of 'divorce' where one live partner is left for another.[44] The Madagascar fish eagle, however, has an unusual family structure: groups of three to five adult birds, with multiple females, multiple males, or even multiples of both sexes.[45] Eagle nests are called 'eyries' or 'aeries' (from the Old French *aire*, which means 'lair'). The distinguishing characteristic of many nests, especially those of larger birds like the golden eagle and sea eagles, is that their nests are often very large and tend to be built high off the ground: in trees and on cliffs in natural land-scapes, or on hydroelectric towers and other tall, remote structures in human-altered landscapes. If there are no high places avail-able, some eagles, such as golden eagles in the southern deserts of the United States, will nest on the ground; but they still require the open space necessary to have excellent lines of sight: eagles like a view. Smaller eagles tend to build less substantial nests that have to be rebuilt each year: Wahlberg's eagles in Africa, for example, build smaller, more temporary nests and may have a few of them in the same area at one time, so they can switch nests on occasion.[46] Eyries are made of sticks, weeds, sod and assorted organic materials and they can be used for decades. Some are massive: since nests are often 'renovated' annually they tend to

Bald eagles on a beach in Alaska. Their nest is located close to the shoreline.

increase in size over the years. The nests of bald eagles tend to start at about 5 ft across and 2 ft high, and there are reports of nests being almost 10 ft across and 20 ft high after years of inhabitation. Similarly, the nests of white-bellied sea eagles in Australia can be enormous, more than 12 ft square.[47] Sometimes eagles will take over the nests of other birds, using them as a kind of prefabricated structure that they renovate in the following years.[48] Many eagle species bring greenery to the nest; this practice has fascinated ornithologists for years and they still are not completely sure why the birds do it. It may be that some types of leaf have insecticidal properties that discourage mites and other pests, thus a kind of pest control is maintained. But it also seems that gathering and arranging the green leaves is some sort of pair-bonding behaviour, like bringing gifts or setting up house in human couples.[49]

Eagles usually lay one or two eggs a year, some as many as three, although when they lay more than one the subsequent egg is often intended as an 'insurance egg' in case the first is not fertilized or is otherwise damaged. In many species if two or more chicks are hatched, there may be an instance of siblicide (also called 'cainism'), where the first-hatched chick, having a head start and being stronger than its sibling, kills the second chick, often in front of an indifferent parent. Cruel as this seems, it is necessary to the well-being of both the first chick and its parents, as feeding each chick places a tremendous metabolic burden on the parents, often causing them to lose weight.[50] With African crowned eagles the hunting rate of the male may more than double to accommodate the nutritional requirements of the newly hatched family.[51] Siblicide is disturbing for human observers, but it may be essential to the evolutionary survival of eagles, a way of ensuring that the surviving chick is the highest quality bird with the most chance of survival.[52] It is also observed that siblicide tends to occur more frequently if food is scarce; in times of plenty multiple chicks can survive.

It takes anywhere from about 60 to 100 days for eagle nestlings to start flying, at which point they are called 'fledglings'. Eagles are careful and attentive parents; they separate out softer bits of food for the eaglets at their smallest stage and patiently feed the largest and most demanding fledglings. Both male and female birds incubate the eggs and tend to the young. There may be some gender division in the family work – the males often hunt while the females brood and guard the young – but this is not a hard and fast rule. Eaglets grow amazingly fast; a bald eagle nestling might gain 6 oz a day.[53] Although an eagle fledgling may be close to adult size, it is often still dependent on its parents for a period while it gains flying and hunting skills; a golden eagle

Charles Livingston Bull, *Eagle with Chicks*, early 20th century, charcoal.

fledgling, for example, needs its parents' help for about 200 days – the better part of a year.[54] While in the nest, the chicks develop hunting skills through playing with inanimate objects and, if the parents provide it, small live prey that has been brought to the nest. Although there are often stories of eagle parents actively coaching their young to fly, or alternatively, callously throwing the young out of the nest to encourage flight, neither habit seems to be true: fledglings are left to find their own way through the process.

Although a juvenile eagle is roughly the same size as an adult, its build may be configured slightly differently from that of a fully adult eagle and its colouration is often different. Juvenile eagles may also engage in somewhat different behaviours than adult eagles; some juveniles are migratory while adults of the same species are non-migratory, for example, or they may migrate to different locales. The juvenile stage can last a long time – several years in some species – with adult colouration and sexual maturity being reached by the age of five or six. The lifespan of many eagle species can be quite long: birds in captivity have lived into their late forties, and recently a banded bald eagle was determined to be 32 years

Bald eagle chicks in their nest on Kodiak Island.

and 10 months old. The oldest bald eagle in the wild documented thus far, it might have lived some years more had it not been hit by a car in 2010.[55] Eagles have to be long-lived to reproduce as a species: given their frugal egg output, the tendency towards siblicide, the long period in which the young require parental support and the high mortality rates of juveniles, it has been estimated that it can take as long as ten years for an eagle pair of the larger species to successfully produce two offspring that live and, in turn, breed successfully. Smaller species seem to have more young, and may not be as long-lived. [56]

The long lives of eagles may have inspired some of the folklore about their wisdom, since we humans tend to assume that if you have been on the earth for a while, you have learned a thing or two. In truth, it is difficult to know how an eagle thinks and any of the core human principles of intelligence are confused by ethical judgements that do not apply to birds. The issue of a parent bird allowing one chick to kill another, for example, might be interpreted as callousness or stupidity by human observers when in reality it is neither of those things. We are learning that birds in general have a great deal of what we might call intelligence, but gauging eagle intelligence is restricted to passive observation, and eagles, when not threatened, tend to be shy and keep their distance from people. There is some indication that they are quite smart. One researcher reports that Steller's sea eagles, who hang around fishing ships for scraps, could tell the difference between familiar fishermen and strange researchers. The eagles would not come near when a team of researchers tried to take advantage of the proximity of the birds to the boat; spotting the strangers, the birds stayed away. What is more impressive is that the birds continued to stay away even when the researchers disguised themselves as fishermen; the eagles clearly 'recognize us individually and by things more subtle than clothing', the researcher concluded.[57]

And eagles may have long memories for individuals: another researcher found that a female white-tailed sea eagle recognized him after a year's absence.[58] But at least one researcher suggests that sea eagles like the white-tailed and Steller's, though smart, may not be the smartest of the eagles. Eagles like the African crowned eagle and the harpy eagle, both of which prey on primates, must of necessity be intelligent: 'you don't learn to outsmart monkeys without being on the ball, crafty and perceptive'.[59]

Outside of family life, eagles have a variety of social interactions with their own species, although they are generally not flocking birds. As a very broad rule they tend to be the least socially cohesive of all the raptors, which, excepting vultures, are not a social bunch as a whole. Only a few eagle species will form flocks of more than ten birds, and then usually for migration or in specific feeding situations. Overall, sea eagles are observed to be more social than some other species.[60] They will congregate with other eagles where there is a large food source, such as rivers where fish are spawning, but these behaviours, called 'gregarious roosting', are contingent upon the food source. In British Columbia and Alaska bald eagles are famous for their gregarious roosting during the salmon run, as are Steller's sea eagles on the northeast coast of Asia.[61] For the record, a large assembly of eagles, be it a case of gregarious roosting or flocking proper, is referred to in English by the rather wonderful expression 'a convocation of eagles'.

We don't tend to think of eagles as migrating birds unless we are fortunate enough to live in one of the 'bottleneck' passages of migration routes. Perhaps we don't think of eagles as migrating birds because we tend to associate that activity with large and visually exciting flocks of birds, such as blackbirds, geese and sandpipers, whose departure and arrival provide crisp seasonal cues to our own patterns of life. Eagles are subtler than this; if they flock at all their groups are small, usually ten birds or fewer. Of the raptors that do form 'super-flocks' (flocks of 100 birds or more) only two eagle species are represented: the lesser spotted eagle and steppe eagle.[62] Most eagles tend to follow the established migration paths that run up and down the continental masses of the earth. Eagle migration can be confusing because the tendency to migrate varies greatly, sometimes even in the same type of bird. Not all eagle species migrate, and even within one species not all birds do it. In fact, sometimes the same individual bird will migrate one year and then not the other. In some species, such as the bald eagle, migration is determined in part by the stage of life; younger birds, 'subadults' up to about the age of five, are far more likely to migrate than adults.[63]

Only four eagle species are 'complete migrants', where more than 90 per cent of the birds will travel. About fifteen other species, including the white-tailed, bald, Steller's sea, imperial and golden eagles, are 'partial migrants', where fewer than 90 per cent migrate every year. Steller's sea eagles migrate away from frozen bodies of water that limit their fishing opportunities, as do bald eagles. The number of 'irruptive and local migrants', where some birds will migrate and some won't (and usually over shorter distances), represents the highest group of eagle species.[64] The tendency of eagles to migrate, as well as the style of migration, is determined by the availability of food, which is in turn determined by the weather and prey migration. In the north a frozen landscape limits food supply; bodies of water freeze over, snow covers burrows and small animals stay under cover. Furthermore, since prey itself migrates southward, away from the cold, it makes sense for many eagles to move south as well. Even in more temperate climates where freezing is not an issue, prey movement can compel raptor migration. In Florida, for example, where there is a large number of bald eagles, the fish tend to 'migrate vertically', going deeper into the ocean during the summer so as to stay cool when the surface of the water heats up. For obvious reasons, this interferes with a surface hunter like the eagle, so the birds tend to move northward in the summer to where the fish are closer to the surface. The bald eagle also responds to fish life-cycles, congregating upriver where salmon go to breed at seasonal intervals. Whatever the circumstances of migration, riding the thermals allows eagles to travel faster and to expend less energy with less flapping and more gliding. This automatically means two things: they migrate during the day and they usually avoid travelling over large bodies of water (only three species willingly travel more than 100 km over water).[65]

Wherever eagles go they have a significant impact on their environments. As top predators and carrion eaters they perform dual ecological functions, managing prey populations and cleaning up organic matter. Whenever eagles cross paths with humans the experience is memorable for the person, and probably also the eagle. Unfortunately we do not tend to have as benign an effect on eagles' lives as they have on ours, and the story of human–eagle interaction is often a sad one. This is strange, for we seem to have a highly developed psychological connection – one might even say dependence – on eagles.

2 Sacred Eagle: Mythology, Religion and Folklore

In his book *Birdscapes*, Jeremy Mynott asks 'Why are birds so good to think with?'[1] For me, this quirky question somehow captured a truth about eagles that I had long intuited but could not articulate; yes, I thought, we use eagles to *think with*. In their complex and wide-ranging roles in mythology and folklore eagles are not simply characters in stories through which we explore our cosmos; they also act as a sort of mental syntax – providing not just a set of ideas, but a way of structuring those ideas. We use eagles to think about some of the most important aspects of our world: the sun, for example, or rain, or death. Eagles represent divine knowledge, light, wisdom, healing, and spiritual or parental guidance, but they also represent divine anger, darkness, storms, sacrifice, war and weaponry. Both sun and storm symbolism connect eagles to the most powerful of god forms; they are often associated with the highest-placed deities in a pantheon, such as Zeus, and in patriarchal cosmologies they are accordingly connected to the higher-ranked male gods and father-gods. Thus, they even have associations with Jesus Christ. Their associations with major gods form connections between eagles and kings, emperors, entire cultures, communities and countries – something we explore in more detail in the next chapter. We use eagles to structure our ideas about existence: the complex and even contradictory nature of eagle mythology is a

An eagle bearing away a fish, and an eagle burning away its plumage near the sun, from an English bestiary made at Peterborough Abbey or Canterbury Abbey, c. 1200–1210.

subconscious recognition of the complex and contradictory nature of that existence.

Eagle spiritual references are so prevalent throughout the world that it is difficult to claim that any particular area is more likely to refer to eagles than others, but the Middle East is especially rich with raptor lore – eagle lore specifically. This is surely due to the fact that it 'sits squarely in the great migratory stream that links Eurasia and Africa',[2] so that in addition to the resident species that live there year round, the area sees many species passing through seasonally. Some suggest that eagle mythology radiated out from early Middle Eastern cultures to the rest of the world;[3] it seems equally likely, however, that while Eurasian mythologies of eagles may have migrated, convergent traditions also developed independently around the world, including in the

Americas and Oceania. The eagle is such an impressive figure in just about any ecology that there is no reason to doubt that creative people all over the world attach similar kinds of significance to it.

One art historian, Rudolf Wittkower, speculated that eagles were among the first objects of worship in primitive religion and that they represented the sky.[4] Although the proof of such speculation has been lost to prehistory, we know that eagles appear as sun symbols in the ancient Near East: the wings on the winged sun discs of ancient Mesopotamia are often assumed to be eagle wings. An Assyrian relief of the sun god Shamash, currently residing in the British Museum, shows the three elements of eagle-related sun iconography coming together: the god is in the centre of a solar disc with eagle wings and tail feathers. Mesopotamian worship influenced Egyptian, Greek and Roman beliefs, all of which involved eagle symbols that were somehow connected to the sun.

The eagle as solar symbol can be found around the world, including in many North American Native traditions, South American indigenous traditions and Australian aboriginal traditions. Since eagles are believed to be able to fly closer to the sun than other birds, they are seen to access the sun god or the highest-ranked god in a pantheon.[5] Usually this is a male god, and it is interesting to note that in most circumstances eagles are associated with male characters, masculinity and paternity. Only occasionally are mythological eagles female: an example is found in Huichol mythology from central Mexico, where the Eagle Mother is the mother of the Sun.[6] Often even the nurturing eagle parent portrayed in folk tales has a rough paternal character that extends to the gods it represents. The classical writer Aelian (c. AD 175–235), who collected stories about every known living thing in his world, has several entries on eagles. He relates a commonly held belief in the classical era that parents tested their young for the ability to stare directly into the sun:

He plants them, while they are still tender and unfledged, facing the rays of the sun, and if one of them blinks, unable to endure the brightness of the rays, it is thrust out of the nest . . . If however it can face the sun quite unmoved, it is above suspicion and is enrolled among the legitimate offspring, since the celestial fire is an impartial and uncorrupt [sic] register of its origin.[7]

Stories like this about eagles pushing chicks out of the nest, which are inherited from earlier writers like Pliny the Elder and Aristotle, are very common and may be attempts to explain the presence of dead chicks found below eagle nests, in reality probably the victims of siblicide.

It is possible that the association between the Greek god Zeus (in the Roman pantheon, Jupiter or Jove) and eagles first rests in Zeus' role as a sky god – soaring eagles may have inspired the connection. Zeus' role as the god of thunder and lightning has also extended to his symbolization in the eagle, which is often depicted with a thunderbolt in its claws.[8] The Greeks assumed from this association that eagles could not be hit by lightening, and some say they attempted to protect themselves from strikes by burying eagle wings on their property,[9] although little archaeological evidence of this has been found.[10] The thunderbolt association was linked to the eagle's role as the agent of Zeus' divine judgement, a symbol and a role often extended to the Judeo-Christian god. The thunderbolt also symbolized weaponry in general and thus eagles are often associated with weapons and war.[11]

The eagle was the messenger of Zeus; early in the *Odyssey* we see Zeus send two eagles to indicate his support of Telemachus' defiance of his mother's parasitic suitors.[12] The eagle is often used to represent Zeus' righteous anger or sexual aggression. When Prometheus transgresses against the gods by giving humankind the secret of fire, his punishment is to be chained to a rock in hell and have his liver ripped out by an eagle every day.[13] When Zeus falls in love with the beautiful youth Ganymede, the eagle kidnaps the boy and takes him up to the god.[14] In Ovid's *Metamorphoses* the god turns himself into an eagle and does his own snatching; Ovid adds the detail that Ganymede becomes the cup-bearer for the gods on Mt Olympus.[15] The star constellation of Aquila is sometimes imagined as the celestial transformation of Ganymede. Elsewhere Zeus' eagles reflect his wisdom or divine knowledge: in order to determine the centre of the world, Zeus has one eagle fly from the east and one from the west, their meeting point being ascertained as the centre of the world.[16]

The connection of Zeus' eagle to both sun and storm imagery is a common paradox in eagle mythology. Some have suggested that the traditional Middle Eastern and Asian association of giant birds with storms has extended to folk beliefs as far as Wales, where eagles are said to predict or even be the cause of storms.[17] The paradox of eagle symbols representing both sun and storm may be due to a more generalized, unconscious recognition of pure environmental power. Both sunlight and electricity are obviously sources of light and power. Alternatively, the connection between sun and storm may be simpler; human consciousness can so easily grasp a thing and its direct opposite together: darkness and light, night and day, creation and destruction. As an extension of the sunlight and lightning symbols, eagles are also associated with fire, which itself is an ambiguous entity, creative and destructive, generative and destructive.

In North America the best-known eagle symbols connected to storms are the Thunderbirds of native culture. Found in First Nations traditions throughout the United States and Canada, the Thunderbird is envisioned both as a huge eagle or other raptor, as well as being its own, purely spiritual, entity. Thunderbirds

(or Thunderers) control the rain and weather, and are the focus of many important spiritual ceremonies; they are said to cause thunder with their wings and lightning with the flashing of their eyes. The northwestern coastal nation of Quileute believed that the Thunderbird lived in the blue glacier of a mountain named Mt Olympus by colonizers – creating an unintentional, but perhaps apt, parallelism with classical eagle mythology. The Iroquois thunder god Hino had two eagles to help him, the golden Keneu (associated with lightning) and Oshadagea (Big Eagle of the Dew), who sprayed water from the lake he carried on his back onto areas that were struck by the fire spirits.[18] In the Iroquois narrative we see the polarity of eagle symbolism – fire and water in this case – neatly encapsulated. Eagles often inhabit the middle spaces of life and death, in the liminal zones between the world of the living and the world of the dead. In the Zuni and Hopi nations there is the story of Eagle Boy in which a boy with a special bond with eagles is taught to fly. He uses his flying skills to visit a city of the dead, which the eagles have forbidden him to do. He gets stuck in this horrific world of living skeletons and the eagles rescue him, but then expel him from their community for violating their prohibition against contacting the forbidden realm.

In another common cross-cultural motif, eagles are often believed to have privileged access to heaven, an otherworld or the realm of the dead. Eagles were believed by the Romans to carry souls to the realm of the gods, and they are frequently represented on Greek and Roman tombs.[19] During the funerals of Roman emperors, eagles were ceremonially released to take the soul up to the gods. The eagle's role as intermediary between the worlds of the living and the dead is seen in Prometheus' punishment of having his liver ripped out by an eagle on a daily basis, effectively placing him between the realms of life and death. He is eternally dying, and the eagle is the agent of this liminal state.

Rembrandt van Rijn, *The Rape of Ganymede*, 1635, oil on canvas.

In this Roman
mosaic Ganymede,
the beautiful Trojan
prince, is abducted
by Zeus in the
guise of an eagle.

With the idea of special access to the realm of the dead or the
realm of the gods comes the idea of special access to knowledge,
especially divine knowledge of the world and its workings. From
this, many corresponding associations for eagles emerge that
frequently intersect with other important elements of their mythologies. The ideas of visual perception connect to mental perception:
clarity of sight is aligned with clarity of mind, therefore the eagle
is associated with intelligence, wisdom, judgement, spiritual acu-
men and, from that, the ability to solve problems, hence, to heal.
The idea that eagles possess deep intelligence and spiritual or
moral awareness might also be inspired by the brooding brow
ridge of many eagle species. The contemplative nature of the eagle
was often drawn from the idea that the eagle's supposed ability to
stare at the sun indicated a superior spiritual insight, or a pure
heart: 'Fearlessly the eagle looks the sun in the face, / As you can
stare at eternal brightness if your own heart is pure.'[20]

The thirteenth-century scholar Bartholomeus Anglicus, in his encyclopaedia *On the Properties of Things*, connected sight to mental clarity. The eagle, he wrote, can look into the sun directly, 'withouten any blenchinge of the eÿen' [without blinking the eyes], this 'spirit of sight', he continued, 'is most temporat and moost scharpe in act and dede of seynge' [most prudent and most incisive of act and speech].[21] This link between visual perception and mental acuity traditionally links the eagle with the fields of philosophy and mathematics.[22] In *The Assayer* Galileo compared philosophers (well, *good* philosophers) to eagles:

> I believe that they fly, and that they fly alone, like eagles, and not in flocks like starlings. It is true that because eagles are rare birds they are little seen and less heard, while birds that fly like starlings fill the air with shrieks and cries, and wherever they settle foul the earth beneath them.[23]

The imagery of light and the theme of superior insight are extended to a spiritual context in the case of St John the Evangelist. His symbol is the eagle, which is commonly found incorporated into church lecterns, especially in Anglican churches: the lectern at Peterborough Cathedral is a famous example. The use of the eagle on the pulpit invokes not just the evangelist himself, but through his larger function as a messenger, God's wisdom as well; the pulpit is the place from which the message takes flight.[24] Thus in Christian iconography the eagle fulfils many of the positive mythological functions we see with eagles in other traditions; it acts as an intermediary between human and god, a bringer of light and a bird of insight.

Insight, however, can be conflated with foresight, and Greeks and Romans subscribed to a theory of divination based on observations of bird behaviour (*ornithomancy*). Observers of birds were

Detail of St John in a window designed by Edward Burne-Jones in 1874, originally in St James Church, Brighouse, now in Cliffe Castle Museum, West Yorkshire.

called *augures* or *auspex* (as in 'auspicious'), and eagles were seen as particularly auspicious birds, in a class called *aves alites*, which meant their flight behaviour formed the basis of the divination.[25] The specifics of bird divination are lost to us, although the practice seems highly subjective: the location of the birds and how they behaved were part of the message.[26] They were said to be able to foretell war (perhaps because as carrion birds, they would have been associated with the battlefield) and are often considered bad omens through this association. But, ever paradoxically, they were also seen as positive omens, able to foretell the birth of important men, especially rulers and leaders. For example, the father of Midas, king of Phrygia, had an eagle appear to him while ploughing, which was a sign of the boy's future regency.[27] Eagles were said to fly in circles over the shrines at Delphi (and indeed there is a healthy eagle population at Delphi, but probably not because it is the centre, or navel, of the world as the Greeks believed, but because of the thermal currents in the mountains).

St John the Evangelist with eagle experiencing an Apocalyptic vision, from *The Grandes Heures of Anne of Brittany*, c. 1503–8.

There are a number of references to eagles as omens in the *Iliad* and *Odyssey*, although the epics also reflect some natural scepticism about augury in general: 'There are lots of birds under the sun', one prophet quarrels with another, 'and not all of them are omens'.[28]

Connecting to the idea of the eagle as a source of insight and foresight is the idea of the eagle as a healer or possessing healing properties, which is somewhat surprising for a bird that is essentially a predator and a scavenger. The Greeks believed in the medicinal properties of just about every bird, and eagles were certainly a part of this tradition. Eagles were said to have magical stones in their nests called eaglestones or *aetites*, which were said to protect the eggs from premature hatching and which would, likewise, prevent miscarriages in women.[29] These stones apparently rattled when you shook them, and the association with pregnancy may have been, as Pliny noted, due to the fact that they appeared as if the stone was 'pregnant' with another stone.[30] In medieval and early modern England these stones were tied to the left legs of birthing women to ease their delivery.[31]

The sharp-eyed bird was also supposed to be able to help with human eyesight: Aelian recommends mixing eagle's gall with honey for a salve to improve vision.[32] The Buryat of Siberia called the eagle the 'first shaman' because it carried sacred healing knowledge.[33] In Indian legend an eagle was said to have brought Soma, the drink of immortality, from the sky to the god Indra.[34] It is interesting how much eagle-orientated healing is connected to virility, fertility and childbirth: eagle blood was apparently an early Viagra equivalent and eagle droppings were said to cure barren women.[35]

Many Native spiritual traditions in North America incorporate eagles into sacred ceremonies and healing rituals, for example in medicine bundles, which are totemic objects used in spiritual ceremonies by individuals to symbolize their connection to the spirit world. Eagles are associated with the invention of the medicine wheel (a sacred site in a circular shape, used for rituals) through the Apsáalooke (Crow) story of Burnt Face, who invented the medicine wheel during a fast. Burnt Face (so named because of scarring from a childhood accident) has a vision in which he sees a tornado turn into an eagle. It takes him to its home where the man's face is healed. The man then helps the eagles by protecting them from otters that eat their chicks and a reciprocal relationship between eagles and humans ensues.[36] The eagle in North America was almost universally seen as a powerful spiritual entity working on behalf of humanity; Cherokee and other nations honoured the great bird in Eagle Dances and other rituals. Eagle figures, carved, stuffed and painted, protected homes and communities in many indigenous cultures.

The connection between healing and eagles is linked to concepts of balance in the natural world, and there is a particular strain of eagle lore that addresses cosmological balance very directly: the motif of the eagle and the serpent, which is found all over the world. Eagle-and-serpent stories extend from the Middle East and Western Europe, through 'Central and South America, Melanesia and Polynesia . . . also Bali, and also in New Zealand, where there are no snakes'.[37] While some have posited that this is a singular cultural motif that has migrated throughout the world from earliest Mesopotamia, it is just as likely that the legends arose independently in different cultures. Eagles frequently do prey on snakes – snake eagles make it their specialty, of course – and the sight of two such intimidating animals in conflict could hardly fail to inspire cosmic visions.

In Mesopotamian symbolism the eagle and snake motif abounds. In Sumerian and Babylonian mythology there is the story of Etana, in which an eagle and a serpent try to coexist in a

Tribal member Will
Tushka carries in
the Eagle Staff
during the grand
entry at the 37th
Annual EBCI Pow
Wow.

Fred Matt, NAFWS
executive director,
carries the Eagle
Staff during the
opening of the
30th Annual
National
Conference
of the Native
American Fish &
Wildlife Society.

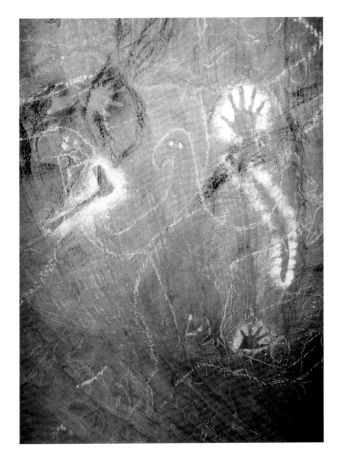

sacred tree. For a while they get on, but it all falls apart when the eagle eats the serpent's children. The god Shamash agrees to help the snake take revenge and tells it to hide in a bull corpse. When the bird comes to feed on the carrion the serpent attacks it, cuts its wing feathers and throws it into a pit. The second part of the story focuses on the infertile king Etana, who is sent by Shamash

Marble relief of eagles, snakes and hares from Constantinople, 10th century AD. Motifs of the eagle/snake and the eagle/hare appear frequently on Middle Byzantine sculptures.

to the eagle trapped in the pit. The two help each other: Etana rescues the eagle from the pit, and the eagle says he will find Etana the plant of birth, in hopes of providing an heir for the king (another incidence of healing by an eagle, who is himself healed in turn after his rescue). The bird tries to carry the king up to heaven to obtain the plant of birth, but three times they are unsuccessful. Eventually the king gets to heaven on the back of the bird and, although the text is unfinished, his quest for an heir is apparently fulfilled, for in the Sumerian king list Etana is succeeded by a son.

An extension of the eagle and serpent topos is the less-frequent tradition of eagles fighting dragons, mentioned, for example in Pliny.[38] Many suggest that the eagle and snake motif represents the union of sky-powers and earth-powers. This can be seen in the case of the sacred world-tree in Norse mythology, Yggdrasil. In this mythical ash tree that holds the world (and eight other cosmic realms), there is an eagle at the top and a serpent in the roots, echoing the Etana story. In the Yggdrasil stories passed down in both the *Poetic* and the *Prose Edda*, a squirrel runs up and down the tree carrying insults between the eagle and the serpent. The eagle on Yggdrasil also has a hawk perched between its brows.

Eagles are found in other 'tree of life' mythologies, for example in the indigenous Siberian Buryat culture, where they are often paired with serpents at the root of the tree.[39]

The eagle and serpent motif may represent cosmic balance or, alternatively, a struggle for dominance between good and evil. It could also have meanings in regard to fertility or sexuality, making it 'of deep psychological significance as well as cosmic meaning'.[40] Even if the symbol is about the relationship between heaven and the underworld, sky and earth, sun and moon, or light and darkness, we should not presuppose that the underworld, earth, moon and darkness should be read negatively. As complex a symbol as the eagle is, the serpent is even more so; snakes are symbols of the beginning of the world, life and regeneration.[41] Therefore the image may not be of two oppositional forces (with eagles on the side of the good), but of a layering up of all cosmic powers, especially generative powers, as both animals are symbols of regeneration. The eagle and serpent motif may perhaps recognize the abstract concepts of dichotomy and opposition that themselves rule human lives; perhaps the specific meanings of each animal are less important than the broader concepts of cosmic struggle and balance. Therefore we must not be too cavalier about imposing simplistic readings of this complicated symbol: its complexity may be the very point. It is interesting that many depictions of eagles struggling with snakes show the battle in progress: the cosmic battle is eternal and unresolved.

Given the eagle's role in nature as a scavenger and predator, it is perhaps surprising that there are not more negative representations of eagles in mythology. The few instances where eagles are villainous tend to be stories where they snatch people away. In Norse mythology the evil giant Thjazi changes himself into an eagle and snatches the beautiful goddess Idunn. Another Norse giant, Hræsvelgr, also takes eagle form and causes the wind to blow with his wings.[42] In addition to these villainous eagles there are many divine transformations into eagle form by gods and heroes of mythology; in Welsh mythology the hero Lleu Llaw Gyffes changes into an eagle to escape an assassination attempt.[43]

Many of the categories associated with eagles – sun and storm, wisdom and danger, healing and death – are contradictory and yet connected, so perhaps it is appropriate that eagle spiritual lore often intersects with purely mythological beasts: monsters, fantastical animals and hybrid beings like the Roc, the phoenix and the gryphon. Mythological eagles are often giant eagles; it seems we are compelled to imagine these large birds as even larger in mythical stories. Or perhaps the stories are not all completely imaginary – the Maori stories of Te Hokioi, or a giant eagle, may well have been based on cultural memories of the Haast's eagle. Around the world, tales of giant birds often seem to figure eagles, or parts of eagles, as their inspiration.

In one of the earliest examples, Anzu, a hybrid Mesopotamian god dwelling in the mountains with the body of an eagle and the face of a lion, was associated first with forces of good and then

The eagle eating a snake symbol is frequently depicted in many cultures. This mural, *Eagle and Snake of the Mexican National Emblem*, by Jean Charlo is at San Ildefonso College, Mexico City.

in later tales he became a figure of chaos. Anzu is symbolically connected to storms and water, but also to the sun.[44] In the story of Lugalbanda, Anzu is a benevolent figure who assists Lugalbanda after this hero feeds the god's fledglings; the rewards Anzu grants Lugalbanda include 'speed of sunlight, the power of storms', both clearly within the usual purview of an eagle figure.[45] In later stories Anzu is a demon who steals the Tablet of Destinies from the gods, which makes him all-powerful. The warrior-god Ningirsu is sent to vanquish Anzu: the figure of the lion-headed eagle then becomes a symbol of Ningirsu, who was the god of war, fertility and vegetation.[46] Agriculture in the Mesopotamian Delta depended on annual flooding, so fertility is linked to thunderstorms. In Sumerian Anzu was called Imdugud, and was associated with other water and weather figures like Inanna

A fragment of a medieval tapestry, c. 1450, found in Basel. Here the mythical gryphon interacts with humans.

(goddess of thunderstorm and rains) and Enki (a water god). Imdugud spread his wings to darken the sky and bring rain to drought-stricken areas.[47] In the case of the early Mesopotamians, the 'roar' of thunder supposedly inspired Anzu's lion face.[48]

Eagles are also frequently conflated with mythological animals like the phoenix, the Avalerion and the gryphon. In Icelandic lore Gammur, a giant bird described as an eagle or a gryphon, is one of the four protective spirits of the island: it drives away cosmological and earthly attacks. In medieval bestiaries, the eagle is often symbolically aligned with mythical birds like the phoenix, especially in its supposed ability to regenerate itself. A thirteenth-century manuscript describes the self-regeneration of the eagle thus:

> When it grows old, its wings grow heavy and its eyes cloud over. Then it seeks out a fountain and flies up into the atmosphere of the sun; there its wings catch fire and the darkness of its eyes is burnt away in the sun's rays. It falls into the fountain and dives under the water three times; at once its wings are restored to their full strength and its eyes to their former brightness.[49]

The eagle's regeneration in this passage might be the result of an imaginative leap from watching the birds hunt fish, with their diving and soaring flight. In the medieval Christian imagination it is read as an allegory for spiritual rebirth or baptism, figured through a reversal of the normal ageing process:

> So you, old man, whose clothes are dark and the eyes of whose heart are darkened, should seek out the spiritual foundation of the Lord, and lift the eyes of your mind to God, who is the font of justice; and then you will renew your youth like the eagle.[50]

This regeneration motif was transferred from Hebrew contexts, such as '[The Lord] satisfies you with good as long as you live, so that your youth is renewed like the eagle's' (Psalms 103:5).[51] In related imagery, the eagle is also a symbol of ascension, especially the Ascension of Christ.

The eagle references in the Bible seem to borrow from eagle mythologies in various Middle Eastern traditions, including Mesopotamian myths of the giant bird Anzu, which may have developed into the Hebrew cosmic bird, the Ziz, mentioned in the Psalms and the Midrash texts.[52] While the Middle East is famed for its falconry and its veneration of hawks in the form of Horus and similar deities, eagles are by far the most common raptor referenced in the Bible, and all of the references seem to envision wild, not tame, birds. The eagle is sometimes conflated with the gryphon vulture in the Bible, which also happens in Mesopotamian and Levantine traditions.[53] Many of the references to eagles in Christian texts are primarily metaphorical, not mythological, but eagle references in Revelation, and in association with the apostle John, have more totemic resonances.

The apocalyptic visions in Ezekiel and Revelation of the four living creatures both include an eagle; these beings represent animate creation and are seen as visions of the power of God. In Ezekiel (10:14) they appear to be composite beings: 'And every one had four faces: the first face was the face of the cherub, the second face was the face of a man, and the third face was the face of a lion, and the fourth face was the face of an eagle.' In Revelation (4:7) they have four distinct bodies: 'On each side of the throne are four living creatures, full of eyes in front and behind: the first living creature like a lion, the second living creature like an ox, the third living creature with the face of a man, and the fourth living creature like a flying eagle.' Either way, the emphasis on their vision indicates their all-seeing power: they are forms of

The four Evangelist symbols in The Book of Kells. Top right is the eagle symbol, associated with St John the Evangelist.

angels and they accompany the throne of God.[54] In the Apocrypha, a monstrous eagle with twelve wings and three heads mentioned in the second book of Esdras is said to represent the Roman Empire's devastation of the Jewish population in the first century AD.[55]

As with pre-Christian mythological associations of eagles from the Middle East, biblical references to eagles are associated with divine power, kingship, sun, storms and death; again they represent positive and negative extremes. In Isaiah we see eagles associated with rebirth or renewal: 'But they who wait for the Lord shall renew their strength, they shall mount up with wings like eagles.'[56] Eagles are sometime associated with God himself, although in a much more diffuse way than with Zeus or other high-ranking male gods. In Deuteronomy God's parental function is highlighted through eagle imagery: 'Like an eagle that stirs up its nest, that flutters over its young, catching them, bearing them upon its pinions, the Lord alone did lead him, and there was no foreign god in him.'[57] In Jeremiah (49:16), however, eagles symbolize human hubris in the face of God's vengeance: 'Though you make your nest as high as an eagle's, I will bring you down from there, says the Lord.' Other negative visions of eagles in holy scripture are connected to the bird's role as scavenger: this is probably the reason for the prohibition on eating eagles in Leviticus.[58]

Often, however, eagles simply provide crisp imagery for the writers of the Bible, especially for comparisons to speed and power, such as 'In life and death they were not divided; they were swifter

Ivory relief carving in Cologne, Germany, first half of the 13th century, depicting the Four Evangelists. St John is represented as the eagle in the top-right corner.

the eagles, they were stronger than lions.'[59] But perhaps one of the most poetic eagle references in the Old Testament comes from Proverbs (30:18–19), which mediates on the humbling beauty of our existence: 'Three things are too wonderful for me; four I do not understand: the way of an eagle in the sky, the way of a serpent on a rock, the way of a ship on the high seas, the way of a man with a maiden.' Religious allegory aside, this passage articulates the gratitude of any eagle-watcher who finds the sight of the soaring bird 'too wonderful', whether they attribute it to the work of God or the work of nature.

Before European colonization brought Christianity to the Americas and to Australia, many indigenous cultures had highly developed religions that also used eagle symbolism. Aztec temples and sacred spaces, as well as those of earlier, related cultures like the Toltecs, are rife with eagle figures and winged hybrid figures that probably reference eagles.[60] During human sacrifice rituals, Aztecs placed the hearts of their victims in bowls carved

Albrecht Dürer, *The Opening of the Seventh Seal and the Eagle Crying 'Woe'*, 1496–7, woodcut. In Heaven, God is distributing trumpets to seven angels, below which a crying eagle flies to earth.

George Catlin,
*Stu-mick-o-súcks
(Buffalo Bill's Back
Fat)*, 1832.

'The Eagle, the
Snake, and the
Cactus in the
Founding of
Tenochtitlan',
from the Tovar
Codex, attributed
to the 16th-century
Mexican Jesuit Juan
de Tovar, which
contains detailed
information about
the rites and
ceremonies of the
Aztecs (also known
as Mexica).

into eagle and jaguar statues that represented the sun and night
respectively; the word for these large sculptures was *cuauhxicalli*,
or 'eagle bowl'; the victims were called 'eagle men'; their hearts
were called 'precious eagle-cactus fruit'.[61] Eagle feathers were one
of the attributes of the highest-ranking Aztec god Huitzilopochtli,
although they were not exclusive to him. Huitzilopochtli, however,
was the god who directed the Mexica Aztecs to the island in Lake
Tetzcoco – where they founded their great capital city Tenochtitlan

(now the site of Mexico City) – with the vision of an eagle on a cactus, so the eagle feathers in his representation may have extra significance.[62] In addition to its connection to Huitzilopochtli, the eagle was connected to the Aztec sun god Tonatiuh. Ritual Aztec drums were also carved with eagles and Eagle Warrior motifs. The Eagle Warriors were elite fighters of the Aztec world and wonderful carvings of these figures still exist: a striking one depicts a man wearing an eagle cloak and a headpiece with the dramatic curved beak of the bird.[63]

As in European cultures the association between eagles and martial activity is a common one among indigenous Americans. The famous war bonnets of the Plains Indians are perhaps the most dramatic example of this. But eagle references in First Nations cultures in North America were as much about peace as war. Around the Great Lakes the Iroquois nations formed the Iroquois Confederacy, establishing as their symbol the Tree of Peace, which has an eagle at its top, on the lookout for danger to the alliance.

In Georgia there is a rock effigy mound in the shape of an eagle that was built over a thousand years ago by the ancestors of modern native peoples; of obvious spiritual significance, its exact function is unknown today. Among the West Coast Native Americans, eagle features are included in monster-type totemic figures that are animal-human hybrids. Bird figures – eagles, hawks and ravens – often contribute beaks to artistic and architectural representations. For example, it is common to have a huge beak structure mounted over the doors of longhouses (functioning as a canopy as well as symbol), and eagles are often represented on painted boxes and other objects. The beak in these images represents 'something other than a creature of the natural world; a being whose multiple attributes suggest multiple identities, whose compound forms suggest metamorphosis or transformation'.[64] The eagles of the coastal nations are also totem animals of clans and moieties; in the social order of the Haida, Eyak and Tlingit nations the eagle was an animal assigned to a moiety, often paired with a raven.

Eagles have similar resonances in Australian Aboriginal cultures. Some of the most pervasive categories of sacred stories throughout the entire continent are the Eagle–Crow stories.[65] The vast network of Eagle–Crow stories spans the continent, but there are some common threads between them that speak to a generalized understanding of the eagle – in this case the wedge-tailed eagle – as a cultural symbol. These stories, which usually feature an antagonistic and yet symbiotic relationship between the eagle and the crow, are partly entertainment (they are often comic) and partly cosmological. They range from naturalistic observations and explanations of the bird's behaviour to cosmological explanations of creation, the formation of water, the place of the constellations and so on. One common story motif explains how crows turned black. In one version, Eagle was being harassed off his kills by crows and decided to exact revenge. One cold day, he placed a bunch of dry sticks in a cave. The crows, which were 'as white as the white cockatoo' at this time, took shelter in the cave:

> Then, by moonlight, Eagle set fire to the crows' bed and burned all their feathers off. When their feathers grew again, they were black, as they have been ever since. The cave is called to this day 'Wocalla an Pindina' – the burning place of the crows.[66]

This kind of story carries a lot of cultural significance, combining nature observation (of bird behaviour – the tendency for crows to harass eagles), mystical explanations for natural phenomena (the crow colour), ethical meaning (the vengeance narrative),

(*Opposite*)
The War Bonnet by Joseph Henry Sharp depicts a traditional eagle feather war bonnet worn by the Plains Indians.

'Gyaana' Haida totem pole, Totem Plaza at Lions Lookout Park, White Rock, British Columbia, Canada. Carved from western red cedar.

Zoological depiction by Wenceslas Hollar of the mythical gryphon, a mix of lion and eagle.

geographical knowledge and history (the naming of the cave). Primarily, however, the Eagle–Crow stories articulate the establishment of the clan, or moiety, structure of Australian Aboriginal society, especially in relation to marriage taboos. Eagles cannot marry eagles; crows cannot marry crows; the cross-breeding from moiety to moiety is explained through the complex, mystical and often irreverent sacred stories.

The characterization of Eagle in these stories is wildly fluid – he is both a hero and a villain – but it is interesting to note that, as in so many other cultures, Eagle is associated with the sky and manhood. It has been posited that Eagle represents the hunter-father, while Crow, a smaller and more mischievous bird often seen raiding eagle kills, is the upstart son. As in other cultures, Eagle is also connected to water and storms. In the form of a 'clever man' or medicine man, Eagle takes all the water from a lake (mythically, the only lake) and carries it in pouches up to the sky: 'Now, instead of all the water being in one place, rain may fall in different parts of the country.'[67] A Wongaibon storyteller, Fred Biggs, points out other cross-cultural similarities with eagle lore after telling 'The Birth of Eagle'. In this story, long before the first man, Eagle is born out of a flower and a few sheets of bark arranged by two sisters (it is common in native stories all over the world to have beings – even people – exist before humanity) and eventually the baby is adopted by the sisters: 'They took it home and reared it up. It was good company for them. He was Eaglehawk. Very clever. This story was like Mary and Jesus.' Biggs means that, as the first man, Eagle's birth was a form of immaculate conception.[68] Another god in Aboriginal cosmology is Namorodo, a fishing god, who can change into the form of the Australian sea eagle, the white-breasted eagle. The totemic power of eagles in Aboriginal culture is seen in their representation in ancient rock art. An important site called Eagle's Reach in New South Wales contains a powerful painting of an Eagle figure holding a boomerang and an axe. The image of this ancestral being dates back 1,600 years. It is tradition that rock art be continually maintained and developed over generations.[69]

The mythological power of eagles cross-culturally is often enhanced by shape-shifting or hybrid qualities. When the power of the predatory bird combines with the intellectual power of a human, or the various powers of other animals like the lion, the result is often a character of immense cultural significance. The gryphon is a beast with a lion's body and the wings and beak of an eagle. Some of the earliest images of gryphons come from Mesopotamian cylinder seals. Like the eagle, the gryphon is associated with the sun, light and gold in early mythologies; it was said to live in nests of gold and to protect treasures, tombs and palaces. It was adapted by Christianity as a symbol for Christ,

The departure of Triptolemos, shown on an Attic red-figure *stamnos, c.* 480 BC.

probably because of its protective qualities and its hybrid character that makes it both of the earth (the lion) and the heavens (the eagle).[70] According to Greek legend it had a nest of gold and eggs of agate.[71] It often appears in medieval heraldry, as its combined animal referents of lion and eagle were perceived as especially noble. The sphinx is another mythological hybrid that involves eagle parts, at least in some versions. The sphinx in the Persian and Greek traditions has wings that are sometimes specified as eagle wings. The sphinx shares the ambiguous characteristics of the eagle of being both a positive and negative figure cross-culturally.

In Hindu cosmology Garuda is a human-bird hybrid with the head, wings and feet of an eagle. The god Vishnu rides on his back. Garuda's human body is gold and he is sometimes associated with the sun, although he is not technically the sun god. Garuda

Detail from the
Harpy Tomb,
Xanthos, Lycia
(in present-day
Turkey), c. 475 BC.

is a figure of justice who, while born of Vinlata/Vinita, the serpent mother, nevertheless is the sworn enemy of the 'naga serpents'
who kidnapped his mother. Related to Garuda are the Persian
Simurgh and Arabian Roc, both giant mythological birds of eastern mythology that are commonly associated with eagles. The
Simurgh is benevolent; it is a composite being (with the parts of
a peacock, dog, lion and sometimes a man) that possesses healing
powers. It is associated with rain and lives in the tree of life – all
attributes we see in other eagle mythologies. There are tales of
it fostering babies and saving women in childbirth, echoing some
other eagle mythology. The Roc is more predatory, best known as
a threat to Sinbad the Sailor. The Roc is sometimes imagined
as white, suggesting parallels with a white eagle in Slavic lore. In

the story of the three founding brothers (Lech, Čech and Rus) of the Slavic nations, Lech, seeing the white eagle, took it as a sign to found Poland, and the white eagle is still on the Polish coat of arms.

Harpies are also human–bird hybrids – winged women – who are commonly associated with vultures, but also sometimes with eagles. The name 'harpy' means 'snatcher', which is very similar in meaning to 'raptor'. One of the largest and most intimidating eagle species in the world, which feeds on primates, has been named the 'harpy eagle', a name which may have originated either in recognition of the mythologies of harpies or through the etymology of 'harpy'. Harpies are usually evil creatures; they have been known to snatch food from their victims (much like a raiding eagle) or snatch the victims themselves away (similar to a hunting eagle). Nevertheless, they have also been used in heraldry, for example in the coat of arms of the principality of Liechtenstein, where the woman-bird image is called a 'virgin-eagle'.

There are even more examples of eagle hybrids. A non-humanoid hybrid is the hippogriff, a mythical creature produced by breeding a gryphon and a horse; since primarily the eagle parts of the gryphon are transferred to the hippogriff, the beast is effectively an eagle-horse hybrid. The hippogriff is mentioned in Ariosto's *Orlando Furioso,* but perhaps its most famous modern example is in J. K. Rowling's Harry Potter series, in the character of Buckbeak. Meanwhile, of all of the eagle hybrids in world mythology, perhaps the one that takes the hybridity prize is a god of the Olmecs of Mexico, which combined the aspects of a harpy eagle with parts of a caiman, jaguar, serpent and human being; the combined elements of this god allowed it to symbolize the sun, water, earth and fertility all together.[72]

The hybridity, liminality and complexity of eagles in mythology make it one of humanity's most all-encompassing symbols.

Laqabi ceramic
from Syria, 12th
century, depicting
an early sign of
harpy heraldry.

With such a range of potential meanings it is no wonder that many
cultures have made eagles central symbols of their heritage: in
the next chapter we explore how the eagle has become one of the
most common heraldic animal symbols, seen on coats of arms,
military insignia and flags the world over.

3 Patriotic Eagle: Flags, Heraldry and Emblems

As a direct consequence of its predominance in folklore and spirituality, the eagle has a long tradition in heraldry, military emblems and national symbols. Many of the eagle's associations with high honours are attached to folkloric traditions that position it as the ruler or 'king' of birds. The idea of the eagle as the ruler of all birdlife clearly stems from the fact that in most ecological systems eagles are top avian predators. Religious beliefs connect human rulers, especially kings and emperors, to the sun and sun gods and therefore the solar symbolism of eagles conveys regal symbolism in many cultures. Folkloric stories of eagles foretelling ascents to power and imperial success abound – it was predicted that the Roman king Tarquinius Priscus (*reg.* 616–579 BC) would be a great king after an eagle grabbed his hat, flew off, then returned to drop the hat back on his head. Old stories about Alexander the Great, meanwhile, tell of how success in his Persian campaign was predicted from the flight of an eagle.[1]

The links between cultural identity, kingship and eagle symbolism can be seen as far back as the myths of ancient Mesopotamia. The Etana myth is a good example of how eagle lore connects the right to rule with broader cosmological significance; Etana's kingship and lineage are established in the context of cosmic balance (the contest between the eagle and the snake), sin, redemption, justice and healing. In other constructions of

Imperial eagle
on the main portal
of the Palace of
Fontainebleau
in France.

eagles as political symbols the imperial symbolism of eagle lore
is often linked to the proverbial wisdom of eagles, which provides an implicit justification for the right to rule. Stories of eagle
fosterage or other sorts of eagle patronage often figure in tales of
royal or cultural lineage. Among Aelian's many tales of eagles is
the story of the infant 'Gilgamos', who is saved by an eagle after
his grandfather, afraid that the infant would usurp him, has the
boy thrown from a tower: 'Now an Eagle which saw with its
piercing eye the child while still falling, before it was dashed to
the earth, flew beneath it, flung its back under it, and conveyed
it to some garden and set it down with the utmost care.'[2] The
keeper of the garden then raises the boy to adulthood. In a
related idea, Aelian says that he has heard that the Persians are
descended from Achaemenes the Persian, who was said to

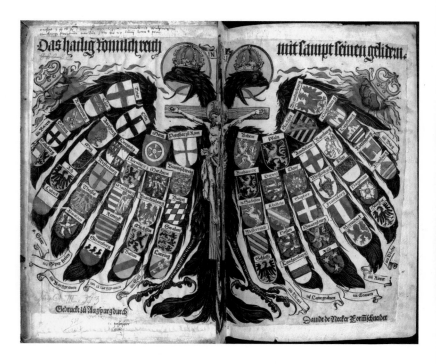

The states of the Holy Roman Empire in a hand-coloured woodcut by Jost de Necker, published in 1510 by David de Necker.

have been nursed by an eagle.[3] In Hungary, the ancient figure of Isten was said to have sent eagles to guide his people into the homeland – what is now Hungary.[4]

The European tradition of using eagles as military emblems also reaches back to Mesopotamia, where they were employed as the symbols of the war god Ninurta/Ningirsu. Single- and double-headed eagles were also emblems of the Sumerian city of Lagash. From these eagles and similar eagle symbols around the Mediterranean comes the most famous ancient eagle emblem, the Roman eagle. According to Pliny the Elder, Gaius Marius, a Roman general, introduced the *Aquila* or eagle standard as the symbol for the Roman army. Pliny explains that before Marius, three other standards were used (the wolf, the Minotaur and the horse), but Marius 'abolished them entirely'. Whenever a Roman legion makes a winter camp, Pliny continues, a pair of nesting eagles will always appear.[5] The Roman eagle standard was not simply an imperial or military symbol for the Romans, it was also a religious symbol. Roman standards, rising high over the heads of the masses, were symbols of a connection with heaven. As the messenger of the gods, especially Jupiter, the eagle portrayed on these standards symbolized connection to the divine realm. Thus these objects were actually worshipped, and there are tales of Roman military leaders throwing the eagle standards into the enemy army, so that soldiers would fight with greater ferocity in order to rescue them.[6]

The Roman *Aquila* is the ancestor of eagle emblems throughout Europe and even, through European colonization that began in the Renaissance, eagle emblems all over the world. Individual rulers in history are partly responsible for the spread of the imperial

Relief with a carved eagle (*Aquila*), symbol of the Roman empire in the Yorkshire Museum, York, a city known in Roman times as Eboracum.

eagle symbol: Charlemagne and the other Holy Roman Emperors used variants of the single-headed eagle that would become the imperial symbol of Germany. The Napoleonic eagle also descends from the Roman eagle; Napoleon had his soldiers carry eagle sculptures on staffs, much like the original *Aquila*. In addition to being employed as a military or imperial symbol, the *Aquila* eventually turned into a common heraldic symbol for European noble families; the eagle first appeared as an official heraldic charge in the early twelfth century, probably in Austria.[7] It quickly became the most common heraldic bird. Heraldic eagles are most often seen in a pose called 'displayed'; this is the term applied to birds of prey on crests with their wings spread. The displayed heraldic eagle is essentially a stylized representation of a real bird in threat display: upright, wings spread, talons forward and ready to strike.[8] Heraldic eagles can also be seen in a variety of other poses, including with folded winds, perched or in various flying poses.[9] Once established in mainland Europe, eagle charges migrated to Britain, where eagle-based coats of arms rapidly

A crowned double-headed eagle of 1723 with the colours of Austria in the choirstall of the parish Church of the Assumption, Waidhofen an der Thaya, Lower Austria.

A late 13th-century Latin translation (known as the *Tacuinum sanitatis*) made in Milan of the *Taqwim al-sihha* (Maintenance of Health) by Ibn Butlan.

gained popularity in the thirteenth century: early in the following century the eagle appeared on more than 40 heraldic crests.[10]

The eagle appears in a famous medieval English heraldic charge, the crest of the Earl of Derby, which incorporates the Stanley family legend of the eagle and child. According to this Lancastrian story, also known as the 'Lathom Legend' (after the Lathom Park estate), Sir Thomas Lathom (*d.* 1370) found his

infant heir in an eagle's nest. The folkloric version of the story
describes how a pregnant Irish queen, under attack by English
forces, fled into the wilderness, where she gave birth to twins.
Fairies stole the female twin and an eagle took the male twin to
England, where he was found by a Lord Lathom in a nest in
Lathom Park. The rescued boy was adopted and put in the line
of succession, finally inheriting the estate. (Cynics say that Lord
Lathom invented the story to legitimize his bastard son.) Eventually
a descendant of this boy married into the Stanley family, and
now the eagle and child legend is part of the Stanley coat of arms.
Pubs have also been named after the story, especially in areas
where the Stanley family held property; the most famous of these
is the Eagle and Child in Oxford.[11]

An important variant of eagle heraldry is the double-headed
eagle. It descends indirectly from Near Eastern cultures such as
the Hittites: the emblem of Rundas, the god of hunting and luck,
was a double-headed eagle with a hare in each foot.[12] Eventually
the double-headed eagle symbol became the emblem of imperial

states like Byzantium. The specific circumstances of the adaptation of the Byzantine double-headed eagle are a bit murky; it was definitely used by the last ruling family of the empire, the Palaiologan emperors, and may have been in use even earlier than that. The symbolic meanings of the double-headed eagle shift according to context. It is commonly assumed to reference the east–west expanse of the thirteenth-century Byzantine empire. Yet the double-headed eagle was also used by the Holy Roman Empire, as well as by Russia and a number of other countries over the centuries, especially in Eastern Europe; in 1993 Russia revived it as its coat of arms. It also appears in English heraldry, often signalling a family's Germanic heritage.

From the standards of armies and the crests of the ruling classes, the eagle moved naturally to national flags, coats of arms and other symbolic functions representing entire countries and cultures. The range of associations attached to the eagles on these flags and national emblems reflects the moral ambiguity often associated with the real bird: representative values for eagle symbols can range from independence and freedom to tyranny

This coin, worth 12 roubles, bears the heraldic device of the Russia's Romanov Tsars, the double-headed eagle.

and oppression. In general, while eagles on contemporary national flags are rare nowadays in comparison with how frequently they were used in the past, they still are very popular on flags of smaller entities like states and cities in Europe. Stemming directly from the aristocratic heraldic tradition of Europe, eagles are also very common in national coats of arms.[13] Most of these heraldic eagles are deliberate cultural referents to the Roman *Aquila*, but some countries, such as Poland and Iceland, get their eagle-related symbolism from folkloric traditions.

Outside Europe eagles are also frequently seen on national flags and coats of arms. As discussed above, the Roman eagle probably descended at least in part from early Middle Eastern and North African cultures that bordered the Mediterranean Sea, so it is not surprising that eagles were simultaneously developing as symbols in Arabian cultures. The twelfth-century sultan of Syria and Egypt, Saladin, apparently had an eagle as his personal

Jack of the President of the Republic of Poland.

emblem. This emblem was adopted by several modern Arab states to signify Arab unity, becoming the coat of arms of the United Arab Republic from 1958 to 1961. The Eagle of Saladin, a left-facing displayed eagle, is on the flag of Egypt as well as the coats of arms of Egypt, Iraq, Palestine, Jordan and Yemen. Syria and Libya changed their coats of arms from an eagle to the Hawk of Qureish emblem, but this is closely modelled on the eagle of Saladin.

Many eagle emblems feature species that are native to a specific country: for example, the harpy eagle appears on the Panamanian coat of arms and the flag of Zambia has an African fish eagle on it, as well as on its coat of arms. Zimbabwe's flag displays a stylized bird figure called the 'Zimbabwe bird', which was based on carved soapstone figures found by archaeologists in the ancient city Great Zimbabwe; the bird carvings are assumed to be of an eagle – either the bateleur or the African fish eagle. In addition to images of real eagles, flags and coats of arms around the world sometimes feature mythological eagle hybrids. Gryphons are common in Europe, and the mythological eagle-hybrid Garuda appears in bird form on the coat of arms of Indonesia, and halfway between his bird and human form on that of Thailand.[14]

An obvious military association with the eagle is flight and it is natural, then, that we see eagles on the badges of many air forces.[15] The U.S. Air Force actually uses eagle symbols in two ways on its insignia, which contains depictions of both the bald eagle and the winged sun disc that goes back to ancient Mesopotamia. Scores of military awards and honours employ eagle motifs, as do associations with quasi-military structures, like the Boy Scouts of America, whose highest rank is Eagle Scout.

Perhaps the most conspicuous national eagles in recent history are the eagles of Mexico, Germany and the U.S.; these three examples exemplify the depth of meaning in eagle emblems

throughout history and serve to remind us of the broad spectrum of political significance that can be attached to the bird. The Mexican eagle, seen on the country's flag and coat of arms, is interesting because it is actually a combination of two extensive mythological traditions, Aztec and European. One of the earliest representations of the Mexican eagle emblem can be found in the Codex Mendoza, a sixteenth-century manuscript produced by the Spaniards to describe what they had encountered in Aztec culture, and it prefigures the Mexican flag of today. The Aztec eagle is seen in the story of Tenochtitlan and in the Eagle Warrior tradition; the image of the eagle on a cactus signals the indigenous roots of the country. But the complex iconography associated with the eagle and serpent also connects it to European Christian culture. Therefore on the Mexican flag the eagle acts as an elegant synthesis of two cultures.

The German eagle has an equally long and complex cultural history. Although heraldry had not evolved by the ninth century, Charlemagne apparently adopted the imperial eagle as one of his many symbols.[16] Since then the eagle has been a common symbol of Germany, albeit one that waxes and wanes in popularity and officialdom as the country defines and redefines its borders. The eagle appears in various forms on German flags and emblems, including as a displayed heraldic eagle, a double-headed eagle (often with a shield combining the arms of states under German control), and various other eagles in flight or ascending on flags, standards, emblems and other forms of iconography. The Germanic eagle – single- or double-headed – is most commonly depicted in a striking black graphic presentation, usually against a gold field (an image borrowed from the Holy Roman Empire). It was common to see the eagle emblem on the *Pickelhaube*, the distinctive spiked military helmets of the nineteenth- and early twentieth-century Prussian army. Modern Germany is a compilation of ancient duchies, states and city states, some of which adopted the eagle and continue to display it much more prominently than

Victorious France, 1809, carved in stone by Antoine-François Gérard, displayed northeast of the Arc de Triomphe du Carrousel, Paris.

the national government currently does. In the mid-nineteenth century there was strong popular pressure for a unified Germany, and the imperial eagle, long used in the Prussian kingdom, was paired with the black, red and gold colours of the current German flag to become a rallying symbol of unification.

In the early twentieth century the black eagle became increasingly popular as a symbol of German nationalism; it was on the state ensign from 1921 to 1933. Before the Nazi rise to power the imperial eagle of the German state (the *Reichsadler*) was a version of the old eagle herald of the Holy Roman Empire. The Nazi version was actually another symbol – the *Parteiadler* (the Party's Eagle). The *Parteiadler* referenced not only the imperial force of Teutonic kingdoms of the past, which were an important part of Hitler's mythmaking, but also Christian, Nordic and neoclassical iconography, which were additional ingredients in

Coat of arms of the Weimar Republic in the 1920s and '30s, which was adopted by the Federal Republic of Germany in 1950.

The eagle is a common fascist symbol. This bird gazed over the Berlin barracks housing Leibstandarte ss Adolf Hitler, the Führer's elite bodyguard.

the mythological soup that Nazis imagined as their cultural past.[17] The eagle fitted in well with the Nazis' extensive use of light-dark imagery, and the eagle's ancient association with the sun was employed to full effect.[18] The National Socialist Party frequently used the eagle in combination with another solar symbol, the swastika. Often the eagle was posed holding a disc with a swastika within it, signalling the rise of German dominance. This image can also be seen in the State Flag ensign of 1935 to 1945. Today the German eagle, which has returned to a version of the *Reichsadler* now called the *Bundesadler* or Federal Eagle, has a quieter function as a cultural symbol; it is still used in military and state symbolism, but not with the high profile that it had in the mid-twentieth century.

The association of eagles with totalitarian regimes like the Nazis is apt to make any eagle lover queasy, but it must be acknowledged. Eagles were prominently used in Italy during the fascist period; the Fascist eagle was an *Aquila* with fasces – a bundle of sticks and an axe-head that represented the power of the state,

On this envelope from the American Civil War era the Union eagle attacks a snake representing the Confederacy. The slogan reads 'The early bird catches the worm'.

another Roman symbol. On the Spanish flag during Franco's dictatorship a black eagle representing St John the Evangelist figured prominently. And in Iraq, Saddam Hussein made ample use of the Eagle of Saladin. It must be noted that most of the eagle symbols appropriated by dictators and fascists originated in cultural heritages that are *not* synonymous with oppressive politics. Still, the eagle as a symbol carries with it an inherent sense of menace that seems to adapt all too easily to tyranny and oppression. As unsavoury as this aspect of eagle lore is, it is important to acknowledge this historical aspect of eagle symbolism. It shows just how quickly our interpretations of eagles can shift from positive to negative, a reality we have seen repeatedly in this study.

The American bald eagle, however, may represent the most prominent contemporary eagle symbol and its history reflects the wide range of emotions eagles tend to elicit. Americans identify the bald eagle with national values related to democracy, individual freedom, national autonomy and military power: many of these associations not only comprise patriotic statements but are often deeply felt on a personal level. Thus the figure of the bald eagle is seen in the United States on all manner of official paraphernalia, but also on every conceivable version of personal statement of American identity, right down to tattoos. The story of how this bird, of all birds, came to be the dominant symbol of American culture and one of the best-known symbols in the world is very interesting, and occasionally amusing.

Like the Mexican eagle, the bald eagle as a national symbol descends from a mixture of European and indigenous influences. The u.s. government followed the European tradition of using eagles as national symbols, so the adaptation of the national eagle is yet another indirect inheritance of the Roman *Aquila* and was part of a neoclassical fashion in eighteenth-century America (the trend is also reflected in the name of the federal 'Senate' and in the architectural style of Thomas Jefferson's neoclassical home Monticello). The shift from the golden eagle to the bald eagle is interesting, however: most heraldic eagles are *Aquila* or booted eagles – fish eagles are comparatively rare in flags and heraldry (Zambia is the only other country that has a fish eagle on its flag and coat of arms). The choice of the bald eagle over the golden eagle is perhaps partly due to Native American influence; the bald eagle had an established tradition as a political and religious symbol in native culture, such as on the Tree of Peace.[19]

The United States adopted the bald eagle as the national bird in 1782. The first person who suggested an eagle as the national emblem was an attorney named William Barton, who had been hired by the committee tasked with designing the emblem. He envisioned a 'small, crested white eagle perched on a pillar above a striped shield', with a sword in one talon and an American flag in another.[20] Charles Thomson, the secretary

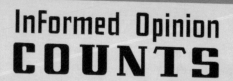

The seal of
the President
of the USA.

of Congress, developed Barton's idea, specifying that the bird
would be a bald eagle and that it would be displayed with its
wings spread, about to take flight. In Thomson's design the objects
that the eagle was holding were changed to a thirteen-leafed olive
branch and a bundle of thirteen arrows (symbolizing the Thirteen
Colonies). He also added a shield-like chevron on the bird's chest
and a banner in its beak that read 'E Pluribus Unum', meaning
'Out of Many, One'. The design then went back to Barton, who
tinkered with the chevron shield and some details of the bird
itself. The process took more than five years until the emblem
was adopted on 20 June 1782. It was first employed as a seal for
official documents, then on items like the buttons of George
Washington's 1789 inauguration suit. In fact, not only did the

A Second World
War rallying poster
released by the
U.S. Government.

eagle symbol represent the newly formed United States of America, but it referred to President Washington specifically. The tradition of associating the eagle with the president is still seen in the Seal of the President and the presidential flag. Eventually it became ubiquitous in daily life, stamped on furniture and every sort of domestic item imaginable.[21]

Not everyone was thrilled with the choice. It was widely noted that the bald eagle was a pirate and carrion bird. Benjamin Franklin famously objected to using the bald eagle in national symbolism in a letter to his daughter on the grounds that the bald eagle was 'a Bird of bad moral Character . . . like those among Men who live by Sharping and Robbing he is generally poor and often very lousy. Besides, he is a rank Coward.'[22] The myth is that Franklin would have preferred a wild turkey and, although this is apparently not quite true, it is interesting to note that the first versions of the eagle on the crest were a little turkey-like: scrawny and unintimidating. John James Audubon also lamented the choice; 'I grieve that it should have been selected as the emblem of my Country', he wrote in 1831.[23] Audubon actually suggested that another sort of eagle, one he named the 'Bird of Washington' or the 'Washington Sea Eagle' (after the president), be used as the national emblem. But the joke was on him, as the bird that he described was in all probability a juvenile bald eagle, which lacks the distinctive white head of the adult bird. The famous ornithologist had been fooled by the dramatic change produced by the maturation process. But the distinctive appearance of the bald eagle won over many enthusiastic supporters for its use as the national symbol. By the late nineteenth century the design had been perfected. A designer for Tiffany's jewellers fine-tuned the design to what we see today: 'its fierce talons, its large wings, its feathered upper legs, its imposing head – more grandly eagle-like and more in keeping with a country poised to assume world

A First World War recruitment poster for the u.s. Navy.

H.S. Matthews
Feb. 1917.

ON GUARD! IT'S A PRETTY BIG JOB FOR ONE BIRD! JOIN THE NAVY!

APPLY RECRUITING STATION OR NAVY LEAGUE

leadership'.[24] A. C. Bent, although an ornithologist who continued to express reservations about the symbol well into the twentieth century, had to concede that: 'Its soaring flight, with its pure white head and tail glistening in the sunlight, is really inspiring', and that 'our national bird may still be admired by those not familiar with its habits.'[25] Others are less reluctant with praise for the bald eagle, both as a bird and as an emblem: John F. Turner, director of the Fish and Wildlife Service under President George H. W. Bush, called it 'a perfect wild symbol of strength and beauty'.[26]

An interesting example of the sentiment attached to the American eagle symbol is found in the story of Old Abe (c. 1861–1881), the much-beloved bald eagle mascot of Union troops from the 8th Wisconsin Volunteer Infantry Regiment. He or she (the sex of the bird is unclear) was carried into battle as a living standard and apparently would adopt a threat pose – wings spread, vocalizing – at the enemy Southern troops. Colourful stories of Old Abe's loyalty to the Union side include one in which the bird flew over the Confederate soldiers, returning eventually to the Union compatriots with the cap of an enemy soldier. Apparently Confederate leaders tried to have the bird captured, but they failed. Old Abe survived all the battles and was retired as a celebrity: dozens of images of the bird survive, often perched on cannons and patriotic regalia, as well as souvenir images and objects. When Old Abe died from smoke inhalation from an accidental fire, there was considerable sadness. Old Abe is memorialized in the insignia of the u.s. Army's 101st Airborne Division, known as the 'Screaming Eagles'. The bird also inspired the logo for the Case Corporation, an agricultural equipment manufacturer.[27] Nowadays the presence of the eagle symbol in American life is so pervasive that citizens 'have become inured to it', according to Bruce Beans:

Stamped on our quarters, half-dollars, dollar bills, and postage stamps, the bald eagle is mounted on homes, storm doors, mailboxes, mud flaps, faux license plates, police badges, and public buildings. It perches atop flag-poles, weather vanes, cheap trophies, and monumental pedestals. It accompanies us from cradle to grave, from the Social Security card we get as infants to the Medicare card we receive upon turning sixty-five, from the u.s. mail to our Internal Revenue Service income tax returns.[28]

A u.s.$5 coin, depicting a Native American on one side and the eagle on the other.

Many states in the union adopted the eagle emblem on their state flags, including Iowa, Illinois, Utah, North Dakota, Michigan, New York and Pennsylvania, as well as the territory of American Samoa.

The American eagle symbol is conventionally thought of as a protector figure, a fierce defender of democracy. The symbol is often used in connection with law enforcement (both local and global) and the enforcement of democratic ideals. Most notably, it is the central figure in the badges carried by members of the

Federal Bureau of Investigation and appears on the seal of the
Central Intelligence Agency. But the ambiguity of the bird's
'moral character' has sometimes undermined that message of
protectionism; the FBI and CIA, for example, are sometimes seen
as predators of their own people and others. In his preface to *The
Scarlet Letter*, written in 1850, Nathaniel Hawthorne meditates

'GOOD HUNTING, SON,—YOU'RE ON YOUR OWN NOW!!!

on the eagle crest above the entrance to the U.S. Custom House in Salem, Massachusetts:

> Over the entrance hovers an enormous specimen of the American eagle . . . With the customary infirmity of temper that characterizes this unhappy fowl, she appears, by the fierceness of her beak and eye, and the general truculency of her attitude, to threaten mischief to the inoffensive community . . . Nevertheless, vixenly as she looks, many people are seeking, at this very moment, to shelter themselves under the wing of the federal eagle; imagining, I presume, that her bosom has all the softness and snugness of an eiderdown pillow. But she has no great tenderness, even in her best of moods, and, sooner or later, – oftener soon than the late, – is apt to fling off her nestlings, with a scratch of her claw, a dab of her beak, or a rankling wound from her barbed arrows.[29]

Nevertheless, the bald eagle is an enduring figure of national pride and endures in the imagination of the American public: in the 2011 Rose Bowl Parade, no fewer than three of the floats featured eagles of considerable size representing American democracy – all made of flowers.

Because they have been associated with kingship and cultural rulers, eagles have sometimes symbolized whole cultures: they become totems of entire peoples, not just the ruler. Real eagles (that is, not just eagle symbols) are often designated national birds or birds of national interest, such as the Javan hawk-eagle of Indonesia, the golden eagle of Mexico, the harpy eagle of Panama and the Philippine eagle of, obviously, the Philippines. In many cases this sort of national affection for eagles works in the birds' favour, as it affords them extra protection under the law. However,

A wood-carved eagle in the Byron R. White U.S. Courthouse, Denver, Colorado.

it can also make them the victims of unsavoury practices, such as their sale as pets or novelty items.[30] In many cases, the national significance of eagles makes them powerful artistic symbols and they have a substantial history in art and literature as allegorical figures, as well as symbols of the power and beauty of the natural world.

4 Aesthetic Eagle: Art, Literature and Popular Culture

The Inupiat-Yupik peoples of Alaska (formerly known as the Eskimo) have a wonderful story about eagles that introduce human beings to the concept of happiness: 'The Eagle's Gift' is about the discovery of community, art and joy. Prior to the eagle's gift, the story goes, humanity laboured in glum, lonely, joyless boredom: 'monotony rusted their minds'. Then one day a young hunter is taken to the eagle's home, where an old mother eagle teaches him the skills of song and celebration which he takes back to his people: 'There were laughter, talk, and sound, and people were care free [*sic*] and happy as they had never been before'. The eagle, by giving story and song, also gives celebration, connection and joy to humanity. The story of the eagle's gift of song is another example of eagles as sources of divine knowledge and higher-order thinking. With the gift of song or art, humanity finds a sense of common purpose and meaning in life. But there is more to the story, for while the people celebrate, the old mother eagle becomes young again: 'for when men make merry, all old eagles become young'. The allegorical message is clear; art, song, literature, celebration and community rejuvenate us, like the eagle.[1]

The role of eagles in art and literature is strange. On the one hand, references to eagles in everyday life are often so common that we cease to notice them, especially if you live in a country like the United States where eagle symbols are ubiquitous. On the other hand, *outside* of contexts related to patriotism or political commentary the amount of art and literature that is devoted to the eagle is relatively scant. It may be, however, that with the pervasive tendency to use eagles as major cultural icons or symbols it becomes difficult to represent eagles neutrally, simply as birds. Paint an eagle, and you've painted a symbolic statement; write an eagle, and you've written an allegory. The domineering symbolism of the eagle is fine if you actually *want* to make a statement or create an allegory, but eagles may be too overpowering for many artists and writers; an eagle in a work of art will steal the show, make it all about the eagle. The same charisma that makes eagles cultural icons also makes them unsubtle poetic subjects; only a few well-known poems are devoted simply to eagles as eagles: one of them is Walt Whitman's 'The Dalliance of the Eagles':

> The rushing amorous contact high in space together,
> The clinching interlocking claws, a living, fierce, gyrating
>   wheel,
> Four beating wings, two beaks, a swirling mass tight grap-
>   pling,
> In tumbling turning clustering loops, straight downward
>   falling,
> Till o'er the river pois'd, the twain yet one, a moment's lull,
> A motionless still balance in the air, then parting, talons
>   loosing,
> Upward again on slow-firm pinions slanting, their separate
>   diverse flight,
> She hers, he his, pursuing.[2]

This breathtaking description of talon grappling eschews obvious allegorizing and moralizing, although it invites contemplation on many things, not the least of which are love, sex, nature and the relationship between animal and human lives. Whitman's restraint is unusual; it is more common to see examples like Alfred Tennyson's 'The Eagle', which combines the observing eye of the birdwatcher with ancient mythological references to the sun and the thunderbolt of the classical eagle:

He clasps the crag with crookèd hands;
Close to the sun in lonely lands,
Ringed with the azure world, he stands.

The wrinkled sea beneath him crawls;
He watches from his mountain walls,
And like a thunderbolt he falls.[3]

The eagle's role in art, literature and popular culture develops directly from its pervasiveness as a symbol and its presence in folkloric and religious cultures, often transmitted through proverbs and sayings. Going back to the classical era we can see writers like Aristotle, Pliny, Aelian and Aesop collecting vignettes about eagles; for these writers, scientific-minded theories about the birds often segue into moralizing proverbs. The folkloric snippets of information compiled by the Roman scholar Aelian are an odd mix of naturalist and mythological content.[4] Aelian's text is a hodgepodge of often contradictory sources, but he is relatively consistent in his representation of the eagle as a noble bird. The eagle is regal and a symbol of purity: 'if one mixes his feathers with those of other birds, the Eagle's remain entire and untainted, while the others, unable to endure the association, rot away'.[5] Still, on occasion he gets caught in the paradox of human admiration and revulsion toward eagles, which he tries to resolve by distinguishing between divine and terrestrial versions

An early 15th-century drawing by Pisanello showing a perched royal eagle.

of the bird: 'The Eagle is a predatory bird; it feeds upon what it can rob, and eats flesh . . . Only the eagle which is called "Zeus's bird" does not touch meat: for it, grass is sufficient.'[6]

Aelian also tells the touching story of a pet eagle which was so loyal to the boy who reared it, 'not as a plaything to sport with, but as a favourite or as a younger brother', that the bird immolated itself on the boy's funeral pyre when the lad died of disease.[7] Aelian further relates the famous tale of Aeschylus, the fifth-century-BC poet and dramatist who apparently died when an eagle dropped a tortoise on him. A witch had earlier told him he would die from having a house dropped on his head (other versions of the tale say the bird was a lammergeyer, a type of vulture).[8]

Of course the grand master of beast fables was Aesop, who was less scientifically motivated and simply spun stories to teach and delight. Many of his examples come from oral tradition and have echoes of ancient myths. The tale 'The Eagle and the Fox', for example, is structurally very similar to the first part of the Etana myth, in which an eagle and a serpent try to coexist in the same tree; in Aesop's version, however, the serpent is replaced by a fox at the foot of the tree. In both stories the eagle kills the offspring of its erstwhile friend. In the Babylonian myth the serpent obtains help from a god; in the fable the fox, powerless to take revenge directly, nevertheless is compensated when the eagle's nest catches fire and the eaglets fall out. In the Aesopian version there is cosmic payback even if the victim can't obtain

The fable of the eagle killed by an eagle-feathered arrow, an illustration from the 'Medici Aesop' manuscript.

'The Eagle and
the Daw' by
Wenceslaus
Hollar, in John
Ogilby's *The Fables
of Aesop* (1665).

vengeance directly. The fable 'The Eagle and the Scarab Beetle'
evokes the principle of retribution when a scarab beetle destroys
an eagle's eggs after the bird refuses to spare the life of a hare.
Aesop's eagles are often representative of either predatory or
noble people; in some fables, eagles reward men who have helped

them ('The Eagle with Clipped Wings and the Fox' and 'The Ploughman and the Eagle' are two of these).[9]

In perhaps the most famous of Aesop's eagle fables, 'The Eagle Hit by an Arrow', the arrow in question is made from the eagle's own feather. This frequently retold story contains multiple, but similar, morals: from 'the pangs of suffering are made more poignant when we are beaten at our own game',[10] to 'we often give our enemies the means of our own destruction'. This proverb was frequently revisited by later writers; the unlucky playwright Aeschylus, for example, refers to it as a Libyan fable in *Prometheus Bound*:

Zeus (Jupiter), with an eagle by his side, holding a royal sceptre and winged Nike (Victory), in the Hermitage, St Petersburg.

Damiano Mazza,
The Rape of
Ganymede,
c. 1575.

So in the Libyan fable it is told
That once an eagle, stricken with a dart,
Said when he saw the fashion of the shaft,
'With our own feathers, not by others' hands,
Are we now smitten'.[11]

In the seventeenth century the poet Edmund Waller picked up this proverb in a mock-courtly poem about listening to a woman sing one of his own songs:

114

Zeus with eagle
on a black-figure
Laconian cup,
c. 560 BC, now in
the Louvre, Paris.

Bertel Thorvaldsen,
*Ganymede with
Zeus as Eagle*, 1817,
a Neoclassical
group in marble.

That the eagle's fate and mine are one,
Which on the shaft that made him die
Espied a feather of his own,
Wherewith he was wont to soar so high.[12]

Whether the lady's rendition was especially beautiful or especially terrible we do not know.

Classical poets routinely drew on traditions of eagle augury, as well as more general associations between eagles and divinity; references to Zeus were especially common. There are several instances in Homer's *Odyssey* and *Iliad* where Zeus sends eagles as omens: in one dramatic scene in the *Iliad*, for example, an eagle wrestles with a snake above the battle between the Trojans and the Greeks, then drops the serpent into the Trojans. This is taken by some as a sign for them to retreat, but Hector is scornful of bird omens and presses on. In the last book of the *Iliad*, the grieving Priam takes the flight of an eagle, 'the dark one, the marauder', as a sign that he should approach Achilles and retrieve the corpse of his son, Hector, who was killed twelve days earlier and was not yet properly buried.[13] In the *Odyssey* the sight of two eagles sent by Zeus is interpreted by the prophet Halitherses as a threat to the predatory suitors of Penelope: 'Odysseus shall not be away from his home much longer', the prophet warns.[14] Similarly, Odysseus is represented as an eagle in a dream that Penelope has towards the end of the saga; in the dream an eagle swoops down and kills her geese, then perches on a roof and declares:

These geese are the suitors,
And I, who was once an eagle, am now
Your husband come back.[15]

The prevalence of classical mythology means that stories like Ganymede and the eagle have long lineages of artistic and literary representation. The Ganymede story, with its intense homoeroticism, has been the inspiration for paintings, sculptures and other forms of visual art for centuries. Although the sexual aspects of the story were often censored, the artistic representations, such as those by Rubens, draw on the erotic (if disturbing) idea of sexual congress with a raptor. Contemporary artists continue to emphasize the tradition of quasi-bestiality (the eagle might be Zeus, remember) around this story; the French photographers Pierre et Gilles took the idea to a camp extreme in their Ganymede series, which features a beautiful naked young man cuddling a (hopefully stuffed) eagle. The grimmer Promethean myth has also attracted writers, dramatists and visual artists from the time of Hesiod and Aeschylus, whose work inspired the Romantic poets Byron and Shelley (who, incidentally, imagined the avenging bird as a vulture instead of an eagle). Franz Kafka listed four versions of the myth in his one-page short story 'Prometheus'.[16] There are a number of versions of the Prometheus myth in visual art featuring the eagle prominently. Perhaps the most famous is Rubens's *Prometheus Bound*, which captures the viciousness of the eagle.

European literature also references a wide variety of eagles unconnected to classical mythology. The eagle, the wolf and the raven were conventionally evoked in early Scandinavian and Germanic literatures as the 'beasts of battle', and as a consequence meant they often became more generalized symbols of death and destruction. This trope was imported to Anglo-Saxon literature in England, as seen in 'The Battle of Maldon':

The fighting was near,
Honour in battle. The hour was come.

Doomed men must fall. A din arose.
Raven and eagle were eager for carnage.[17]

In *Beowulf* the carrion beasts convey the news of their spoils to each other: 'the raven winging darkly over the doomed will have news, / tidings for the eagle of how he hoked and ate, / how the wolf and he made short work of the dead'.[18] In the Old English poem 'The Seafarer', the scream of a sea-spray-soaked eagle adds to the forlorn mood of isolation and despair.[19] There is a nasty Anglo-Saxon curse that reads in part:

Under the wolf's paw, under the eagle's feather
Under the eagle's claw, ever may you wither.[20]

There is an even nastier story of the execution rite called the 'blood-eagle', which was probably spread by misinterpretations of pre-twelfth-century Skaldic poems that actually use such phrases as 'under the eagle's claw'. Accounts of this method of execution contained descriptions ranging from eagle figures being carved into the backs of victims to victims' backs being sliced open and their ribs being broken away from their spine to create a 'spreadeagle' effect. Compounding the horror, some descriptions include the removal of the lungs. It has been suggested that the blood-eagle stories are essentially anti-Viking propaganda; nevertheless, the stories persist.[21]

By the High Middle Ages and Renaissance, however, writers seemed to gravitate towards more positive representations of eagles that they drew from the classical tradition, instead of adopting the grim scavengers of Nordic culture. References to eagles in relation to Zeus were, of course, popular and were adopted into Christian theology by Dante and other writers. There are important references to classical eagle lore in this poet's *Divine Comedy*,

Prometheus Bound, 1618, an oil painting by Flemish artist Peter Paul Rubens that depicts the punishment of Prometheus.

usually connecting eagles with Jupiter, albeit in the context of a
Christian allegory/dream vision. In *Purgatorio*, meanwhile, the
narrator has a dream of being snatched up by a golden eagle
(literally golden, in this case, not just the breed); he is carried up
to a 'sphere of flame' and awakes to find that Lucy, his spirit guide,
is taking him to the gates of Purgatory.[22] In *Paradiso* the narrator
sees the spirits of eight 'just rulers' form the phrase *Diligite iusti-
tiam qui iudicatis terram* ('Love justice, ye that judge the earth';
the first words of the Book of Solomon, the proverbially wise and
just ruler). The spirits then transform the final 'm' of the phrase
into the form of the imperial eagle, which represents justice (there

is an interesting diagram in the notes of Dorothy L. Sayers's translation that shows how this transformation from letter to bird is possible). The eagle then speaks to Dante about the nature of divine justice, and displays lights in one of its eyes that are the lights of six just rulers on earth. Since this all happens within the realm of Jupiter, Dante's eagle connects to the Zeus tradition, as well as to many other symbolic realms of eagledom: wisdom, justice, perception, light and power.[23] The French artist Gustave Doré produced scores of illustrations for Dante's texts, including the eagle scenes from *Purgatorio* and *Paradiso*. (He also depicted the hero of Ludovico Ariosto's epic poem *Orlando Furioso* riding the hippogriff.)

Geoffrey Chaucer had fun with the idea of Dante's eagle in his own dream vision *The House of Fame*. The narrator of this poem, a bookish, retiring sort, is taken on a journey by a golden eagle,

Dante, in a dream, carried off by a golden eagle in *Purgatorio*.

who 'shon so bryghte / that never sawe men such a syghte, / but if the heven had ywone / all newe of gold another sonne.' The solar imagery is obvious, and the role of the eagle as a spirit guide combines the function of the bird as a messenger of the gods with the stories of people being carried away by eagles. In this case Chaucer lends scepticism and humour to the latter aspect, as his hapless narrator first faints in shock, then tries to wriggle out of the bird's grasp; 'Seynte Marye,' snaps the eagle, 'Thou are noyous [annoying] for to carye!'[24] The eagle explains that he is Jupiter's bird, and while he has no plans to carry the narrator to heaven and make him into a star like Ganymede, he will take the narrator to the House of Fame to learn about love, fame and earthly renown.

Cupid and an Eagle by Wenceslaus Hollar after Giulio Romano.

Chaucer used eagles again in another dream poem, 'The Parliament of Fowls', where three male eagles compete for the 'hand' of a female eagle in a courtly debate. This parliament is an extension of the 'king of birds' tradition that stretches back to Aesop and his Asian sources.[25] Chaucer's eagles are divided into two categories: the 'royal' eagle, which probably means the golden eagle, and 'lower' eagles:

> There might men the royal egle fynde,
> That with his sharpe lok perseth the sonne   [*pierces the sun*]
> And other egles of a lower kynde,
> Of which that clerkes wel devyse conne   [*that scholars describe*]

The royal eagle is once more associated with solar imagery and the poem draws on the idea of eagles being able to stare directly into the sun. The royal eagle is characterized as the perfect courtly lover, 'wise and worthi, secre [discrete], trewe as stel [steel]'. He and the other 'lower' eagles embark on a courtly display of chivalric speech and general puffery to try to outdo each other; but when it becomes obvious that their courtly virtues are roughly comparable and that the debate is going nowhere, the other bird species in the parliament become impatient and begin a raucous discussion about the process. Chaucer's humour is heightened by the insertion of zoologically realistic touches regarding the character of the birds. When someone suggests that a trial by combat might be one way to resolve the issue, the eagles reflect their raptor nature: '"Al redy!" quod these egles tho [then]'. Violence is averted and the debate brought to a close when the female eagle, the epitome of feminine gentility, requests an extension of her deadline. This is granted by Dame Nature and it is determined that the decision will be made in the following year – one has the sense, though, that it is the royal eagle's game to lose.[26]

The nobility of Chaucer's symbol is tinged with a gentle humour, stemming both from the idea of talking birds and perhaps also from the irony of the noble eagle – a raptor and a scavenger standing in for the noble classes – specifically. There is some speculation that the royal eagle was meant to represent Richard II's courtship of Anne of Bohemia in 1380.[27] In a way Chaucer anticipates comic representations of anthropomorphic characters like Sam the Eagle in *The Muppets*, combining mythological aspects with zoological detail to produce funny, but vivid, eagle characters.

Shakespeare made full use of classical eagle mythology and ancient folklore, as well as the metaphors that come from those traditions. In plays situated in Rome and in Roman Britain like *Julius Caesar* and *Cymbeline*, the classical eagles of Jupiter, the Roman imperial eagle and ancient theories of bird augury provide a network of cultural detail. In *Julius Caesar* Cassius interprets the fact that eagles abandon the camp as a bad sign; with the noble and protective eagles gone, he frets, 'in their stead do ravens, crows, and kites / Fly o'er our heads, and downward look on us / As we were sickly prey' (v.i.79–86). In *Cymbeline* Jupiter himself makes an appearance, with his eagle by his side, and the eagle of Jupiter is frequently referenced elsewhere in the play. Borrowing from the classical tradition, eagles in Shakespeare are often symbols of monarchy and heraldry associated with England. In *Henry v* the Bard repurposes an old folktale for a political allegory; the Bishop of Ely cautions the King:

> For the eagle England being in prey,
> To her unguarded nest the weasel Scot
> Comes sneaking, and so sucks her princely eggs . . . (I.ii.166–71)

Other ancient folklore motifs also appear in Shakespeare's works, as seen in his references to the proverbial ability of the bird to stare into the sun. In *Henry VI, Part 3*, the future Richard III challenges his older brother to demonstrate his moral right to take their father's dukedom and eventually the kingdom: 'Nay, if thou be that princely eagle's bird / Show thy descent by gazing 'gainst the sun' (I.ii.91–2). Other eagle references in Shakespeare may come from traditional folklore or perhaps simple observation, as when he compares an unruly Roman populace to crows pecking at the senatorial eagles in *Coriolanus*.

Like Shakespeare, Edmund Spenser turned to well-established proverbs regarding eagles, drawing specifically on the idea that the eagle can regenerate itself like a phoenix by diving into the water and then flying back out again. Spenser's *Faerie Queene* illustrates how Christian audiences saw this proverb as a metaphor for baptism, borrowing from Psalm 103: 'Bless the Lord, O my soul, and forget not all his benefits . . . Who satisfieth thy mouth with good things; so that thy youth is renewed like the eagle's'. The hero of the romance-epic, the knight Redcrosse, who represents the English people, is reborn through baptism to defeat the Dragon. While his lady, Una, watched, Redcrosse 'upstarted brave':

> Out of the well, wherein he drenched lay;
> As Eagle fresh out of the Ocean wave,
> Where he hath left his plumes all hoary gray,
> And deckt himselfe with feathers youthly gay,
>
> . . .
>
> So new this new-borne knight to battell new did rise.[28]

Later literature is peppered with eagle symbolism of various kinds. In 'The Canonization' John Donne uses the alchemical term 'eagle', which is apparently one stage on the way to the

Frontispiece to the 1825 edition of the poem *Childe Harold's Pilgrimage* by Lord Byron.

CHILDE HAROLD'S Pilgrimage.

J.H Jones fecit.

Canto 1.   Stanza 39.

IN 4 CANTOS,

LONDON.

Printed & Published by W. Dugdale, Russell Court, Drury Lane.

1825.

transmutation of metals, to construct the idea of the merged divinity of the lovers: 'we find in us the eagle and the dove'. The eagle and the dove is another cosmic pairing of opposites, like the eagle and the serpent, an image that continued to resonate in new contexts in the literary tradition. Shelley revisited the ancient image of the contest between the eagle and the serpent at the outset of his long poem 'The Revolt of Islam'. In a scene reminiscent of the *Iliad*, an eagle appears in the sky, struggling with a snake. The allegorical meanings of the scene are disputed, but the energy in the depiction is unquestionable:

An eagle among other birds, an avium species illustration designed by Francis Barlow and engraved by Wenceslaus Hollar.

> A shaft of light upon its wings descended,
> And every golden feather gleamed therein –
> Feather and scale inextricably blended.[29]

127

While the serpent apparently loses the battle, the eagle is 'exhausted' and his victory is not as glorious as one would expect. As the passage above clearly suggests, the distinction between the two combatants is blurry, and the message seems to be that good and evil are inextricably bound up together. Some have suggested that the eagle also represents Shelley's poetic friend Lord Byron, who also wrote a version of the Prometheus myth, albeit referencing a vulture rather than an eagle. Byron, who was a great animal lover, also kept a pet eagle in his menagerie.

William Blake's work references eagles in several contexts. In the poem 'The Marriage of Heaven and Hell', the section 'Proverbs from Hell' mentions eagles: 'The eagle never lost so much time as when he submitted to learn of the crow'.[30] In the same poem a reference to eagles in the section 'A Memorable Fancy' is an allegory of how books are printed (Blake considered books akin to spiritual objects). In this section he describes the 'third chamber', the realm representing the actual process of etching plates with acid (feathers were used to 'agitate the acid' in the etching process), as a realm of eagles: 'In the third chamber was an Eagle with wing and feathers of air; he caused the inside of the cave to be infinite; around were numbers of Eagle-like men, who built palaces in the immense cliffs.'[31] Blake's cosmology was highly developed and complex, but eagles feature frequently as divine figures: 'When thou seest an Eagle, thou seest a portion of Genius; lift up thy head!'[32] For Blake, 'genius' was a divine animating spirit invested into the world by the ancient poets; thus eagles in this context are connected to art, spirituality and the life force. Blake's 'The Book of Thel' begins, 'Does the Eagle know what is in the pit?', meaning that the eagle really only understands the realm of the sky (the next line indicates that the eagle should ask the mole about life underground).[33] This is interesting as it also seems to echo the Mesopotamian story of Etana, in which the eagle is thrown into a pit after eating the snake's young, although it is unclear whether Blake would have been familiar with this myth.

Authors engage old traditions concerning the divinity of eagles in different ways. T. S. Eliot had a personal view of Christianity that evoked the eagle as an important symbol. The eagle in his pageant play *The Rock* may most directly refer to the constellation Aquila, but its cosmic implications encompass the broader ancient associations between divinity and eagles:

> The Eagle soars in the summit of Heaven,
> The Hunter with his dogs pursues his circuit.[34]

On the other hand, Tennyson, in 'In Memoriam', pushes back against the idea of the eagle as an aspect of a god. Wrestling with belief in God, he declares that he 'found Him not in world or sun, / Or eagle's wing, or insect's eye'.[35]

In contemporary fiction, eagles have considerable presence in the fantasy literature that borrows motifs from ancient folklore.

A section of mosaic showing the Eagle of St John at S. Vitale, Ravenna, c. 546–8.

A grey earthenware raptor-shaped vessel, 36 cm high; Yangshao culture (5000–3000 BC), found in China's Shaanxi province.

In *The Hobbit*, for example, Tolkien's eagles are ancient archetypes from medieval and pre-medieval culture; they are larger than normal eagles and are noted for their wisdom and nobility. They reappear on occasion in *The Lord of the Rings* as shady heroes from the mountains. As already mentioned, J. K. Rowling revived the hippogriff legend in the character of Buckbeak, Harry Potter's favourite mount. She also uses eagles in the crest of Ravenclaw House, harking back to real heraldic eagles of yore. The history of the Roman Empire, especially its impact on Britain, has inspired literature that references the *Aquila* symbol: Jack Whyte's *Dream of Eagles* novel series is one example; another is Rosemary Sutcliff's novel *The Eagle of the Ninth*, recently made into the film *The Eagle*, which tells the story of a legion in Britain sent to recapture the precious eagle standard lost by a troop a generation earlier.

Kishi Gantai, *Eagle and a Monkey*, hanging scroll. An eagle on a rock beneath a pine tree eyes a monkey hiding in a cleft in the rock below.

Because of the tendency for eagles to be overdetermined as symbolic figures, representations of the birds in art frequently fulfil allegorical functions, especially political commentary. A good example of this is found in Leonardo da Vinci's *Allegory of the*

This hanging scroll detail depicts an eagle eyeing his prey in the snow.

Wolf and the Eagle, a rather odd red chalk drawing that features a wolf sailing a boat and a crowned eagle perched on a globe radiating light towards the wolf. The precise allegorical message that Leonardo was trying to construct is still disputed, but the imperial nature of the eagle is clear.[36] It is common to see eagles included in the representations of kings, emperors and other important leaders, often incorporated into the clothing, armour, crests and decorative detail around the person depicted. Statues and paintings of St John including the eagle were also common in medieval and Renaissance Europe, reminding us of the spiritual role of the bird in Christianity. A less common form of eagle-inspired artwork is the Renaissance interest in automata, mechanical artworks of animals, which were apparently sometimes constructed in the forms of eagles. It is reported that the astronomer Regiomontanus invented a flying mechanical eagle: there is an account of it flying to greet Emperor Maximilian.[37]

Artwork from Asia also frequently features eagles. There are several stunning silk paintings and watercolours from China and Japan of eagles; raptors are common subjects on screen paintings.[38] Recently, one such painting by Qi Baishi (1864–1957) fetched an astounding $65.5 million at auction. The Japanese artist Kishi Gantai (1782–1865) painted a compelling portrait of an eagle with a monkey, which is now in the British Museum. This painting was produced during the Edo period (1603–1868), when birds of prey were popular subjects with art patrons from the upper classes, who felt their social power was appropriately reflected in raptor symbolism.[39] In China and Japan eagles are considered heroic animals, like the horse and the lion, and they were used in political allegory by painters of the early twentieth-century revolutionary era in China, such as Gao Qifeng (1889–1933).[40] Interestingly, however, a sixteenth-century Japanese painter named Kanō Utanosuke also saw the eagle as a symbol of Zen

consciousness: 'it seems to be a Buddha among birds', he wrote in a letter.[41] Similarly, the eagle in Asian art has been associated with themes of age and wisdom. In the painting *Eagle in the Snow* by Itō Jakuchū (1716–1800), the crested serpent eagle evokes the aged perspective of the Japanese painter in his eighties, in the winter of his life.[42]

American culture has its own distinctive tradition of eagle symbolism in art and literature that combines Old World references, native traditions and patriotic symbolism. As already mentioned, the two eagle species in the continental USA are the bald eagle and the golden eagle. Of these two, the bald eagle, with its dramatic white head and its status as national symbol, seems to attract the attention of writers and artists more, especially on the coasts where the bird is prevalent. Eagles in American writing frequently symbolize abstract concepts connected to the majesty of the natural world and the place of the individual within it. The eagle is employed as a symbol of freedom on

The U.S. President Woodrow Wilson (1913 to 1921) is perched on his 'Firm Foreign Policy' nest made from 'Protest' letters. William Jennings Bryan leaves Wilson's cabinet in the form of a dove, escaping the dark clouds of 'Possible Trouble'.

multiple levels: the natural freedom of the bird, the political freedom of the American people and the personal freedom of the individual.

American writers frequently evoke the national symbol to discuss politics. E. B. White (the author of *Charlotte's Web*) wrote 'The Deserted Nation' as a protest at environmental damage in the 1960s:

Chemists and farmers flourish at their peril:
The bird of freedom, thanks to them, is sterile.[43]

Mid-twentieth-century writers employed the symbol in their poetics of resistance, frequently personifying the American eagle to critique government policy and social attitudes. In his mid-century Beat-style cri de coeur 'I am Waiting', Lawrence Ferlinghetti writes 'I am waiting / for the American Eagle / to really spread its wings / and straighten up and fly right'.[44] A darker example of 'eagle resistance politics' is found in the graphic novel *Shadowplay: The Secret Team*, by Alan Moore and Bill Sienkiewicz, which is paired with another graphic novel called *Flashpoint* to form the two-book series *Brought to Light: Thirty Years of Drug Smuggling, Arms Deals, and Covert Action*. These books depict corruption in the CIA in the mid-twentieth century. In *Shadowplay* a human-sized, drunk, bitter American eagle spills the beans on CIA corruption; the effect is not comic but rather highly disturbing, as he reveals the thousands of casualties of the Vietnam war, the Iran-Contra Affair and the American government's involvement with Chile and Panama.

Such contrasts between the natural existence of eagles and the violent, corrupt reality of human existence have been employed allegorically to suggest more spiritual or moral comparisons between people and the American national symbol. In 'The Eagle and the Mole', Elinor Wylie encouraged readers to:

Avoid the reeking herd,
Shun the polluted flock,
Live like that stoic bird,
The eagle of the rock.[45]

For poet Carl Sandburg the eagle was a personal symbol affirming his connection to his country and the world in general:

There is an eagle in me and a mockingbird . . . and the eagle flies among the Rocky Mountains of my dreams and fights among the Sierra crags of what I want . . . and the mockingbird warbles in the early forenoon before the dew is gone,

A 19th-century
Tlingit culture
eagle mask
from Alaska.

warbles in the underbrush of my Chattanoogas of hope,
gushes over the blue Ozark foothills of my wishes – And I
got the eagle and the mockingbird from the wilderness.[46]

Texts such as these appropriate eagles as symbols of individualism, producing a somewhat ironic tension with the use of the bird as a symbol of collective American identity.

Some of the eagle imagery in American art and literature is borrowed from the iconography of traditional native artists. In First Nations art, the eagle is frequently represented in highly stylized terms that reference the bird's cosmological function. Paintings of eagle figures in native communities, for example on the painted screens that cover the front exterior walls of longhouses, depict the bird in its spiritual role and its function as a totem animal. On the northwest coast the Pacific First Nations are famous for their 'formline' art, a highly abstracted style of representation in which all of the space is utilized, whether the space is a canvas, a box, a totem pole or the front wall of a building. Contemporary totem poles also continue to use the traditional symbols, including eagles, and active First Nations artists extend these motifs into both traditional and new mediums. In Native literature, spiritual traditions merge with contemporary poetic styles, as is the case in 'Eagle Poem' by Muscogee (Creek) poet Joy Harjo. Birth and death, she writes, are blessings because they happen within a

True circle of motion,
Like an eagle rounding out the morning
Inside us.[47]

Such artistic renderings reflect the ongoing spiritual traditions in native communities and forge links between native and non-native cultures.

With the rise of environmentalism in the twentieth century, many artists have taken on the task of rendering the beauty of the natural world – and the threats to it – in painting, sculpture and film. Eagles frequently play significant roles in 'nature art' where animals are represented realistically. In modern nature art the symbolism of eagles is largely positive, connected to an increased conservation ethos: eagles, often bald eagles, present abstract representations of the beauty, power and freedom of the natural world. One of the most famous artists in this genre is Robert Bateman, whose paintings of eagles are both highly realistic and deeply moving. Although the depictions themselves are taken from the birds' lives and are thus apolitical, the emotional power of the paintings frequently produces an implicit message: we must work to preserve a space in which eagles can simply exist, without interference from humans.

Swoop, the official mascot of the Philadelphia Eagles.

In the United States the federal symbol of the bald eagle is easily expanded to include sports teams. The highest-profile eagle-identified team in the USA is the Philadelphia Eagles of the National Football Association. There are also several minor league teams in American and Canadian ice hockey (such as the colourfully named Cape Breton Screaming Eagles), as well as dozens of college and university sports teams that use eagle insignia. In fact, 'Eagles' tops the list of most-used college sports team names among American schools, including the Boston College Eagles, the California State University Los Angeles Golden Eagles and the Emory University Eagles. In Association football (soccer) 'eagle teams' may be found around the world, including Mali's Les Aigles and Serbia's White Eagles. Some Australian Rules football clubs are named after eagles – at the national level, the West Coast Eagles – as are some rugby clubs.

The use of eagles in American sports emblems connects to the more general cultural and political symbolism of the bald eagle. A cartoonish bald eagle was the mascot for the 1984 Summer Olympic Games in Los Angeles: it was named Sam, for Uncle Sam. This 'patriotic' use of the American eagle has spawned a significant industry in what might be called 'eagle kitsch', which uses the bird to symbolize the shallowest sort of jingoistic sentiment. Posters, T-shirts, coffee cups, statuettes and all manner of cheap tat can be purchased with bald eagles positioned against slogans like 'Freedom', 'Resilience' and 'Honor'; the American flag frequently provides the backdrop. It is this sort of thing that caused American poet Robert Francis to protest in the 1970s that the true dignity of the bird is beyond such tawdry exploitation: 'The American eagle is not aware he is / the American eagle', he wrote; 'If we have honored him we have honored one / who unequivocally honors himself by / overlooking us.'[48] Artist Bettina Hubby took a playful view of the surfeit of eagle paraphernalia in her installation *The Eagle Rock Rock and Eagle Shop* (2012), a temporary store located in the Los Angeles neighbourhood of Eagle Rock that was dedicated to the collection and sale of anything to do with rocks or eagles (including a number of items that fit into both categories).[49]

Other eagle references in modern American history connect to military traditions. This can be seen in instances like the first lunar module to land on the Moon being named *Eagle*, and in Neil Armstrong's accompanying declaration: 'The Eagle has landed' – a phrase that became iconic in its own right. The mission insignia for *Apollo 11* features a bald eagle with an olive branch in its claws landing on the Moon, with the Earth in the background. Other uses of the eagle in American popular culture are somewhat less reverent. On *The Muppets* Sam the Eagle's stuffy patriotism and bourgeois taste in music is played to great comic effect. Sam is a satire on the pomposity of the eagle symbol in American patriotism. He is not fearsome, but rather a middle-class elitist with

The official *Apollo 11* mission patch. *Apollo 11* is the spaceflight that landed the first men on the Moon, Neil Armstrong and Buzz Aldrin, on 20 July 1969.

pretentions to nobility. In popular music the most famous eagle-related entity is of course the rock band The Eagles, started in California in 1971. The history of the band's name is a bit murky, although it seems that Native American influences and the associations of the bird with America lent the band the kind of image they thought appropriate to their ethos and style. Overall, it is tricky to summarize the cultural presence of eagles internationally, but as we have seen throughout this book, positive and negative associations with the bird continue to be mixed together.

A second Alaskan story may have foretold the way these associations would meld. This story follows the tale of the eagle's gift of joy told at the start of this chapter. In this tale another, very similar, episode takes place in which the eagles encourage the young hunter to have a celebration. This time, however, things go wrong; a man who was a 'sacred messenger' is accidentally murdered and an attempt to make amends fails. The feast is spoilt and the dances are confused; the sacred messenger's allies attack the unwitting murderer. This was the first war: 'Thus merrymaking and war succeeded each other,' the storyteller Arnasungak moralizes, 'It could not be otherwise. Merrymaking and gaiety warm the mind; but it is a step from wild exuberance to rash behaviour.' In this story, the eagle's gifts – art, joy and community – also contain all the opposite qualities: discord, aggression and violence. This is an intuitive and artistically deft recognition of the paradoxes of this beautiful, terrible bird. But we are always drawn to these paradoxes, for, as Arnasungak reflects, 'who would exchange the joy of festivity for the intolerable monotony which made life so empty before the eagle's gift?'[50]

5 Eagles in Our World

The ways in which humanity interacts with eagles seem to be largely determined by culture; many cultures and spiritual traditions assign eagles cosmological significance. These cultures, which are often indigenous ones, have a very different relationship with real eagles than that shown by monotheistic cultures with less emphasis on the natural world as a part of their spiritual practice. Another variable in human–eagle interaction is economy and lifestyle. Farmers have different priorities than urban developers, and industrial economies require different infrastructure than traditional subsistence living.

In cultures where eagles have spiritual or cosmological functions real eagles are usually granted some sort of respect. This does not necessarily mean they are not killed: many ceremonies in indigenous communities in Australia and the Americas require eagle sacrifice for religious or cultural purposes, but the killing is sacred, not motivated by a sense of threat or dislike. Some Native communities in North America hunt eagles for feathers and other body parts that are used ceremonially. Although in the past large numbers of eagles were taken, the arduous and ingenious hunting methods necessary before the use of guns tended to naturally limit the kill. A common method was 'pit trapping', where a man hid in a dugout camouflaged with branches or grasses with bait placed on top. The hunter then had to lie still,

A postcard depiction of the Eagle Dance performed by Pueblo Indians in New Mexico.

sometimes for hours, until an eagle landed on the bait, at which point the hunter would grab it through the roof of the structure. He would then suffocate it or break its neck. Wrestling with a panicked eagle required a great deal of strength and courage, and the hunt was highly ritualized.[1] Some nations, such as the Hopi, preferred to take nestlings and raise them in captivity before sacrificing them, but this, too, was a highly ritualized practice. In general, the rituals around sacrificing an eagle were very similar to the rituals for a human enemy killed in battle; the bird's life was considered as sacred as a warrior's life.[2]

Native communities used – and still use – eagle parts, especially feathers, in ceremonies and in traditional dress. Most famous in the contemporary public imagination are the war bonnets of the Plains nations, which used the black and white feathers of juvenile golden eagles.[3] When the Bald and Golden

142

Eagle Protection Act was passed in 1940, a system was set up to distribute eagle parts (the result of roadkills, natural deaths and other non-hunted deaths) to Native Americans who applied for them. Nevertheless, the ceremonial use of eagle parts became one of the most contested issues between Native American communities and the American government. In the late twentieth century a series of court cases involving Native eagle hunters who were selling eagle parts for profit caused a great deal of animosity towards the American government's policy on eagle protection. So too did eagle conservation policies that could restrict how Native communities used their ancestral lands: 'The eagle is valuable', one Tlingit councillor told a researcher in southeast Alaska, 'but people are more valuable'.[4] To this day, Native attitudes towards eagle conservation are conflicted. While many First Nations consider it taboo to kill eagles at all, others

A mounted Kazakh hunter with his golden eagle.

Eagle mask with movable wings, used ceremoniously by the Nootka people of Canada's Pacific Northwest Coast.

War bonnet and trailer on display at Nez Perce National Park.

Cheyenne Peach chiefs Lawrence Hart, Darryl Flyingman and Harvey Pratt at the opening of the Red Earth Native American Cultural Festival, 2008.

consider eagle hunting integral to their spiritual practice and cultural identity; even if they agree with the principle of eagle conservation, they don't necessarily appreciate governmental intrusions in the name of enforcement.

Similarly, in other parts of the world European colonization had a direct effect on how people interacted with eagles. Although eagles had less of a central role to play in most African religions, African indigenous relations with eagles were apparently balanced. Leslie Brown noted that traditional African knowledge included excellent 'field naturalists'. This knowledge was corrupted, he felt, by European influence: 'With modern education . . . most of this old-style field knowledge disappears, and sad to relate, anything with a hooked beak and talons is likely to become an object of enmity'.[5] Traditional Australian native attitudes towards eagles were also largely benign, and while Aboriginal Australians used eagle parts in ceremonies they did not endanger the populations in any significant way. Aborigine hunters would trap wedge-tailed eagles by setting fires (eagles are attracted to smoke because prey can be caught while fleeing a fire), then used a boomerang or spear to fell the birds that came close.[6]

In pre-modern Europe some types of eagle – primarily golden eagles – were used in falconry, although social taboos about rank, as well as the sheer physical size of eagles, made this a rare occurrence. According to Juliana Berner's *Boke of St Albans*, a fifteenth-century treatise on hawking and hunting, only emperors or the highest of kings were permitted to hunt with eagles. It seems unlikely that such rules were closely followed, however: they were perhaps an ideal more than a reality of falconry. Regardless of rank, one would have to be a premier falconer to manage such a formidable bird; if eagles were indeed used by emperors it is likely the actual flying of the birds would be designated to experts.

The Kirghiz and Kazakh people are famous falconers who still use golden eagles on horseback in Central Asia. They hunt wolves, foxes and small prey for food and pelts; they are one of the few cultures (perhaps the only one) in which the quasi-domesticated eagle is integral to their domestic economies. Today these falconers have a healthy side business in tourism, as visitors come to see the eagles in action. Golden eagles hunting wolves have been captured on video, and online images demonstrate the astonishing power and determination of the birds; a single eagle can take down a grown wolf. It is dangerous, however. There is also footage of wolves seizing the birds and shaking them like ragdolls. Amazingly, some of these eagles still manage the kill, although in some scenes it looks likely that both animals are mortally injured. Wolf hunting is more of a novelty for most eagle falconers than it is a common hunting practice; the falconers prefer to keep their eagles for a decade or so and then release them into the wild to breed.[7]

Eagles do not lend themselves to domesticity in the way of some other birds, although there are a few instances where eagles have been tamed. Indeed, American ornithologist A. C. Bent notes that bald eagles 'make gentle and devoted pets' but that they 'require an astonishing amount of food'.[8] A touching (if unverified) story of human-eagle interaction comes from the horrors of the Siberian prison camps in the 1940s, where a Jewish prisoner trained an eagle as a pet, but then had to release her during a winter famine because there wasn't enough food for either the bird or the prisoners. The eagle left, but she returned – and returned repeatedly – with hares and other mammals for the prisoner and his fellows, which helped keep them alive for two more years.[9]

People occasionally eat eagles, although in Europe this happened primarily in the Middle Ages, a time of impressive omnivorousness, when many things were consumed that are no longer considered edible.[10] In Asia eagles are sometimes on the menu today, but it is not a common occurrence. As we have seen, there are prohibitions against eating eagles in the Old Testament, and

Burkut falconers in Kazakhstan, from T. E. Gordon's *Roof of the World* (1876).

other cultures may similarly find the idea of eating a carrion bird off-putting. Also, there is not much meat on an eagle; divested of its feathers, it is often remarked that there is little substance to one of these birds.

Overall, Western cultures have seen little 'use' for the bird. Since colonization eagles in North America, Africa and Australia have been seen as pests and as such have been persecuted, in some cases to the brink of extinction. Large-scale livestock farming sees any predator as a threat to the economy and eagles are often deliberately destroyed. In the United States, Australia and other countries the slaughter was state-sponsored in the early twentieth century, with bounties offered for dead eagles. The numbers of eagles killed were astounding: thousands every year. Alaska paid 128,000 bounties between 1917 and 1954. In 1936 a California rancher was paid $700 in bounties – a significant sum at that time. In Australia it is estimated that mid-century kills hovered at around 13,000 wedge-tailed eagles per year in Queensland and Western Australia alone.[11]

Shooting eagles was a sport, a civic duty and pleasure for many; even the famed ornithologist John James Audubon was astoundingly cavalier about killing and eating eagles. He described a two-day hunting expedition in 1832, on the St John's River in Florida, in which several young eagles were killed. According to Audubon, young bald eagles 'proved good eating, the flesh resembling veal in taste and tenderness'.[12] In the early part of the twentieth century the most common end for a bald eagle was to be shot. There were even reports of people shooting eagles from planes or helicopters in the western states.[13]

The notoriety of the birds as raiders of livestock is often undeserved, stemming from lore passed down from generation to generation that often goes unquestioned by farmers and ranchers even though eagle attacks on lambs, pigs and chickens

are quite rare. In Australia the wedge-tailed eagle, which is an important part of the ecosystem in a continent without vultures for cleaning up carrion, has been badly persecuted by some ranchers.[14] During the mid-twentieth century rows of dead eagles were strung up on fences by ranchers as a display of their success in the cull. But again, eagles do not have the impact on live-stock populations that many think; when eagles do kill lambs, it has been found that the lambs are often ill or starving.[15] The rate of lamb kills is generally much smaller than supposed: less than 3 per cent of the total lamb crop in Scotland and similar percentages in North America, although in Australia it may be a bit higher.[16] In Scandinavia similar or lower rates of fawn kills occur in domestic reindeer populations, which are also overestimated by farmers.[17] In all likelihood farmers probably overestimate the amount of livestock predation by eagles because

An adult harpy eagle feeding at Miami Metrozoo.

149

they can frequently come upon eagles feeding on the carcasses of stock that has died by other ways; the birds are judged guilty by circumstance.

Hunting eagles has done significant damage to many populations, but just as devastating has been poisoning, both deliberate and accidental. Farmers and ranchers poison eagles for the same reason they shoot them: fear of livestock loss. Farmers sometimes poison eagles by leaving baited animal carcasses for scavengers to find. Sometimes the eagle is the intended target, but just as often the eagle is collateral damage (or a bonus kill, depending on your perspective) when another animal like a coyote is poisoned. The indiscriminate nature of pest poisoning can be devastating: not only eagles and coyotes have been victims, for poisons have done significant damage to prairie dogs, ground squirrels, ferrets, red wolves and the California condor in the western United States. The effects of poison do not stop with the death of one animal, for it produces what American wildlife officials refer to as 'rings of death'. In the early 1990s American federal agents estimated that 2,000 to 3,000 bald and golden eagles were killed each year 'from Texas to the Dakotas by various illegal or restricted poisons'. One official remarked that they 'found enough poison to kill every predator, man, woman and child west of the Mississippi'.[18] Deliberate or secondary poisoning of eagles is a significant problem all over the world: many countries have outlawed poisoning, but it continues to be done illegally.

Sometimes anti-eagle propaganda claims eagles are dangerous to people, but most eagle observers report that the birds are quite shy with humans and will even leave a nest with eggs or young in order to avoid a confrontation. Still, common sense is in order when dealing with these large birds. Generally, if you respect an eagle's space, it has no interest in you. Nevertheless, stories of eagles carrying off people, especially babies, are endemic to many cultures. Some of these are folkloric and have cultural significance, but some purport to be factual. Bent speculates that an eagle 'if pressed for food, might carry off a baby that had been left in the open unprotected', but then notes that 'such an opportunity must occur very rarely'.[19] Indeed tales of eagle attacks on children might be taken with a grain of salt when the only witnesses are the children themselves – a child might be unnerved by a low-flying eagle, but he is unlikely to become lunch. In the nineteenth century such stories abounded, passing into common lore by way of sensationalist stories like 'The Eagle's Nest', which was published in a children's reader.[20] Thomas Edison once made a film that featured a scene of a baby being carried by an eagle, and before D. W. Griffith became a director (of *The Birth of a Nation*, among others) he acted in a film called *Rescued from an Eagle's Nest*, in which he played a lumberjack whose baby is snatched by an eagle.

These ideas of baby-snatching eagles might be due to a misunderstanding of the bird's ecological role. One researcher reports that a piece of a child's skull had once been found in the nest of an African crowned eagle, but that it had likely been scavenged from a corpse.[21] Alternatively, the scenario might be a sort of ancestral memory (if such things can be said to exist) from an earlier time in human history. We have evidence of African crowned eagles taking early humanoid babies: the fossil of the 'Taung Child' (*Australopithecus africanus*) is thought to have died this way.[22] Or it has been suggested that eagle abduction stories may be cultural memories of eagles that are now extinct. In particular, the monstrous Haast's eagle of New Zealand could be the subject of many of these stories. It killed giant flightless moa birds and so surely was physically capable of killing a person (although some researchers express doubts that it ever did so).[23] Of course, there is some danger of people being attacked by captive

Painting of a golden eagle flying off with a lamb. Famous ornithologist James Audubon depicts himself in the lower-left corner.

The Eagle and Child is a pub in St Giles, Oxford. The name is based on folkloric stories that tell of eagles stealing sleeping children. The pub has associations with the Inklings writers' group, which included J.R.R. Tolkien and C. S. Lewis.

eagles, since they can never truly be tamed, but blame for this must be laid on the handlers. Overall, eagles are no real threat to people.

Obviously we are more dangerous to eagles than they are to us, even when we don't mean to be. Accidental poisoning often results from medicines fed to livestock animals. India and Pakistan have seen significant losses of eagles and other carrion birds, such as vultures, because cattle are being treated with drugs that cause kidney failure in the birds. Traditionally, cow carcasses have been left for scavengers. Hindus do not eat meat and Muslims require that it be specially butchered, so usually cattle die of natural causes or accidents and are left to rot in the open air. Until recently it was a good arrangement between human and raptor, but now the dead cattle are toxic. Similarly, mice, rats and other vermin that are poisoned and thrown in rubbish dumps also hurt scavenging eagles. Accidental poisoning of eagles can also occur through things like the lead in bullets used to kill other animals. In America lead shot was outlawed for waterfowl hunters in order to save bald eagles that would otherwise eat the lead along with purloined birds, but in other places, such as north-eastern Russia and Asia, birds such as Steller's sea eagle are still endangered by lead poisoning.[24] But by far the most insidious form of incidental or accidental poisoning of eagles has come from the use of DDT, other pesticides and chemical pollutants.

In the late 1940s and '50s American eagle watchers noticed a steady and dramatic decline in eagle populations from year to year. Very few chicks were being hatched: when conservationists climbed to the nests of eagle pairs, they would find no eggs at all or, more often, fragments of eggshells. It took the conservationists a number of frustrating years to determine the cause, but when they did it proved to be a pesticide called dichlorodiphenyltrichloroethane, or DDT. Developed as a pesticide in Switzerland in 1939, it was first used to control mosquito populations in areas being occupied by Allied troops, to prevent the spread of malaria. It became a civilian product in 1945 and was found to be equally effective against common agricultural pests like cotton boll weevils and potato beetles. DDT found its way into the food chain. It does not break down in the body, but is passed from prey to prey up the food chain, becoming more and more concentrated in the bodies of each successive predator. At the top of the food chain are the eagles and other raptors, so they suffered some of the greatest effects. The primary effect of DDT on eagles was egg-thinning: the eggs would crack under the weight of the brooding parent. Among the worst affected were the fish eagles, since the aquatic food chain is long and pesticides reached very high levels in fish before the eagles took them. By the 1960s raptor populations were in crisis. The numbers of the white-tailed eagle in the Baltic Sea were declining rapidly, as were the bald eagles in North America. Eventually, in 1972, DDT was banned from most of its American uses, although it was not banned in other countries, such as Australia, until more than a decade later.[25] The effects of DDT and other organochlorines may persist in long-lived species like eagles, so we may not have seen the last of its effects worldwide, but since its use has been reduced, the numbers of bald and white-tailed eagles have rebounded (in conjunction with many other conservation initiatives).

Currently the greatest threats to eagles all over the world are habitat loss, pollution and climate change. Next to pesticides, the most significant chemical threat to eagles are PCBs (polychlorinated biphenyls), dioxins and other industrial pollutants. The primary impact of these toxins on eagles seems to be birth defects: an unusual number of birds with crossed bills were found in the Great Lakes region of North America in the early 1990s. White-tailed eagles in Sweden were also found to have an increase in crossed bills and foot defects, and PCB contamination of the Baltic is thought to have been the cause.[26]

On top of all of this there are numerous accidental deaths: our modern lifestyle can be unintentionally hazardous to eagles. Many eagles are hit by cars while feeding on roadkill, and structures such as utility poles and wind turbines can also be deadly. Occasionally there are collisions with aircraft and helicopters.[27] Many birds can safely perch on power lines because they aren't grounded. Large birds such as golden eagles, however, are big enough to touch two wires at once with their wings, thus conducting a deadly current.[28] Power lines have especially damaged the population of Spanish imperial eagles, whose distribution is restricted to a small range.[29] Conservationists all over the world have started to work with power companies to lessen the impact on eagle populations; sometimes a design modification to equipment or a more sensitively positioned power source can make significant improvements to bird survival rates.

All over the world, contemporary forestry practices, large-scale agriculture and urban development are causing habitat loss, especially for woodland birds. In South America the rainforest is being decimated by logging operations at an astounding rate. The massive harpy eagles, as well as the solitary eagles, are threatened by this activity. Eagles that are island dwellers or that live in smaller ranges are especially vulnerable to habitat destruction as there is simply nowhere for them to go once the restricted environment on which they depend is gone. The most obvious example of this dilemma is seen in the two Madagascar eagles that are found nowhere else in the world. For years the small Madagascar serpent eagle was thought to be extinct. A small number have been found, however, but they are still highly threatened by deforestation of the island, where slash-and-burn agriculture is the modus operandi for Malagasy farmers. The situation in Madagascar reflects a common scenario in environmental issues; the needs of desperate people are pitted against the needs of the eagles. Conservationists attempt to strike a balance between people and eagles, since most communities actually do value their resident eagles and will adapt practices to protect them.

A restricted range like an island may make eagles vulnerable, but so too does a large range that takes eagles over different borders and different environments. Some areas that migrating birds pass through on their journeys are inhospitable (as deforestation and other land augmentations deprive them of resting places and food sources) or downright dangerous (as the birds pass into territories where they are hunted). Cross-border treaties are required to solve these problems and such negotiations are often politically fraught. International conservation treaties, furthermore, are not well enforced from border to border.

Madagascar fish eagle (*Haliaeetus vociferoides*) at Antananarivo Zoo, Madagascar.

Eagle conservation and protection programmes are managed by interlocking networks across the globe. There are international programmes like the Convention on International Trade in Endangered Species of Wild Flora and Fauna (CITES), which specializes in the monitoring of animals and animal parts across borders, restricting the flow of trade (legal and illegal) of endangered animals, including several eagle species. The European-based International Union for Conservation of Nature (IUCN) is an umbrella network that supports hundreds of conservation projects involving animals of all types, including eagles. It publishes the 'Red List' of the most endangered plant and animal species. Currently there are three eagles listed as 'critically endangered': the Madagascar fish eagle, the Flores hawk-eagle and the Philippine eagle. (The Peregrine Fund in the United States also lists the Bawean serpent eagle as 'critically endangered'.)

Individual countries host a variety of protection programmes, some of which take an interest in threatened animals far beyond their own shores, such as the American-based Endangered Species Act, which was established in 1973. Programmes run by governments – regional, national and international – have the advantage of a higher public profile and more enforcement powers. When the Bald and Golden Eagle Protection Act was enacted in the United States, its mandate included not only the protection of the birds but also public education about their magnificent national symbol. In both objectives the Act was highly successful, and bald eagles were removed from the Endangered Species List in 2007.

Non-profit organizations like Birdlife International, its partner the Royal Society for the Protection of Birds (based in the UK), and the Peregrine Foundation (based in the USA) can try to step into the breach when government will or resources are lacking, and these networks do oversee dozens of conservation initiatives all over the world. We have a vested interest far beyond birdwatching in keeping eagle populations healthy. Eagles are beneficial to all the ecological niches they inhabit, including the ones they share with humans. They keep down the population of pests such as rodents, snakes and undesirable fish species. As do all major predator species, eagles also tend to prey on weakened animals, removing them from the line of descent. As carrion eaters, they dispose of carcasses that could spread disease. In many cases we need not only to prevent eagle deaths, but also to encourage more eagles to be born. Most species of eagle are fairly long-lived and slow to reproduce, so some conservationists tip the odds in the eagles' favour to create optimal breeding conditions. There are programmes that provide safe nesting sites: in some places platforms are constructed along power lines so that the eagles which would otherwise risk electrocution by attempting to nest on the pylons have safer options. Another method of encouraging eagle population growth is called 'hacking' and involves taking the eggs or very young nestlings from a nest and raising them partially in captivity, in order to re-release them into the wild when they are mature enough to survive on their own.

Hacking and captive breeding programmes of other kinds can be used to minimize things like the siblicide that can occur in the wild. Removing one of the eggs to be hatched in captivity eliminates the risk that one chick will kill the other (which is a common occurrence), and allows more eaglets to survive from each clutch. Similarly, the second, weaker chick may be rescued from a nest to prevent siblicide, as has been done in Spanish imperial eagle and Madagascar fish eagle conservation. Conservationists also sometimes remove all of the eggs from a nest so that the parents will produce a second set that season – this is called 'double-clutching'. Fostering has also been used on select eagle populations. Once the chicks have reached a certain age, the risk of siblicide diminishes, so new chicks (or chicks that were rescued earlier) can be added to a nest. Although it does increase the burden on the parents, fostering can sometimes be worth the extra work.

Conservation programmes around the world can count some successes. The golden eagle population in Europe is getting healthier, although there seem to be persistent problems with poisoning, shooting and habitat destruction in the United Kingdom, despite laws protecting the birds. Reintroduction programmes for the white-tailed eagle have been initiated in Scotland and are showing some success. The Spanish imperial eagle, the European cousin of the golden eagle that had been decimated by hunting, electrocution and deliberate or pesticide poisoning, has made a slow

Wedge-tailed eagle (*Aquila audax*) chomping on a frozen rat at the Lone Pine Koala Sanctuary in Brisbane, Queensland.

climb back from only 30 breeding pairs in the 1960s to more than 200 breeding pairs now.[30] The Madagascar serpent eagle, once thought to be extinct, is currently listed as endangered (one step away from 'critically endangered'). Population estimates for this species vary from a few hundred to around a thousand birds – better, obviously, but still not enough to ensure the species' survival long-term. Its island brother, the Madagascar fish eagle, which seems naturally to have a very small population, is also threatened by persecution and deforestation. All large forest eagles, especially the harpy eagle and Philippine eagle, are in trouble due primarily to habitat loss, and the recent interest in these birds may have negative as well as positive outcomes; they are sometimes hunted for trophies or trapped for exotic pets. Conservationists have been working to save these astounding birds, but since both species require very large hunting territories to survive, a substantial effort will be required to protect their habitat.

The Australian states' governments, which once classified wedge-tailed eagles as 'noxious animals', reversed their policy and brought in protective laws in the 1970s with positive results. Where once eagle corpses were slung along ranch fences, now the birds are symbols of national pride. Although habitat loss continues to be a problem, it is to be hoped that an increased awareness of the needs of eagles will balance economic development with habitat protection. Wedge-tails are doing well on the mainland, where they even appear to be able to tolerate fairly close proximity to people, but the subspecies in Tasmania are still in trouble – like all island eagles, their limited geography makes them more vulnerable.

In some ways eagles may have an advantage over other endangered animals because of their tendency to become part of human culture as symbols and mythological entities. It is interesting that, until the onset of modern industrialization, humans and eagles rarely interacted directly: farmer's concerns aside, they rarely compete with us for food (some of the large tropical eagles compete with humans for 'bushmeat', but before the recent destruction of forest habitats there would have been enough for both birds and humans). Eagles are difficult to catch and not usually considered good eating, so for most of human history eagles have lived their lives and people have watched from afar. And watch them we did: we watched them and we spun stories around them, for perhaps the greatest interaction between humans and eagles is in the realm of imagination. Eagle lore exists all over the world; eagles are totems, symbols and characters in human cosmologies, and it is in this role that eagles have had the most direct impact on human lives.

Eagles will always fascinate us, and since most people now understand that they pose no real threat to humans or human activities, public perceptions of eagles are generally positive, especially in the West. The long history of eagles as symbols has also helped make them one of the most commonly appreciated birds, even by individuals who have little general interest in ornithology. [134] The eagle tourist industry is alive and well in several areas of North America, where visitors are treated to the spectacular vision of eagle nesting sites, where dozens of the birds may be seen in a cluster of trees. Modern interest in conservation uses modern technology to connect people to eagles in positive ways. In May 2011, for example, viewers watched live online videos anxiously while an eagle chick that had become entangled in a fishing line was rescued by wildlife officers who accessed the nest via a crane (the line was apparently brought into the nest by its parents, along with a fish). While some wildlife experts are wary of nests becoming public knowledge, in this case it helped, since the officers were assisted in stabilizing the cranes in the wet earth by drainage companies that had heard of the young bird's plight.[31] Penny Olsen, the Australian ornithologist, offers a prayerful vision of our future with eagles, which she calls 'birds of earth and ether': 'Long may eagles live beside us unmolested, long may they adapt to our altered landscapes, long may they hold a place in this increasingly humanized world.'[32]

Timeline of the Eagle

145–66 million years BP	4th millennium BC	2000 BC	1000 BC–1000 AD
Cretaceous Period: neornithines ('new birds') appear	Mesopotamian cultures develop eagle, double-headed eagle and winged solar disc motifs that will inspire eagle symbolism to present day	Australian Aboriginal rock paintings of eagles begin	Rock Eagle Effigy Mound constructed in what is now Putnam County, Georgia, USA

4th century	768–814	1240s	14th century
Eagle images painted on Australian cave walls	Rule of Charlemagne, who adopts a version of the Roman *Aquila*	Emperor Frederick II of Hohenstaufen writes *The Art of Falconry* and adopts eagle emblem	Eagle heraldry employed on more than 40 English family crests

1935–45	1940	1945	1958
Party Eagle holding swastika used on State Flag ensign by National Socialist Party of Germany	U.S. Congress passes Bald and Golden Eagle Protection Act	DDT introduced as a commercial pesticide	United Arab Republic adopts Eagle of Saladin for its coat of arms

4th century BC

Aristotle describes six types of eagle in *The History of Animals*

3rd century BC

Aelian writes *On the Nature of Animals*

early 1st century BC

Gaius Marius decrees the *Aquila* to be the Roman standard

mid-1st century AD

Pliny the Elder writes *Natural History*

1308–21

Dante writes *The Divine Comedy*

c. **1382–6**

Chaucer writes 'The Parliament of Fowls' and *The House of Fame*

1782

The USA adopts the bald eagle as its national emblem

early 20th century

Bounties on eagles offered by Australian and American governments

1970s

Laws protecting wedge-tailed eagles introduced in Australia

1972

DDT banned in USA

1973

Endangered Species Act passed in USA

2007

Bald eagles taken off Endangered Species List

References

1 EAGLES THEMSELVES: BIOLOGY AND ECOLOGY

1 Leslie Brown, *Eagles* (New York and London, 1970), pp. 7–8.
2 Colin Tudge, *The Bird: A Natural History of Who Birds Are, Where They Came From, and How They Live* (New York, 2008), pp. 45–53.
3 Luis M. Chiappe, *Glorified Dinosaurs: The Origin and Early Evolution of Birds* (Sydney, 2007), pp. 118–45; Gary W. Kaiser, *The Inner Bird: Anatomy and Evolution* (Vancouver, 2007), p. 174.
4 Casey A. Wood and F. Marjorie Fyfe, trans., *The Art of Falconry of Frederick II of Hohenstaufen* (Stanford, CA, 1943).
5 Michael Walters, *A Concise History of Ornithology* (New Haven, CT, 2003), p. 14.
6 Heather Lerner and David P. Mindell, 'Phylogeny of Eagles, Old World Vultures and other Accipitridae Based on Nuclear and Mitochondrial DNA', *Molecular Phylogenetics and Evolution*, XXXVII (2005), pp. 327–46.
7 Penny Olsen, *Australian Birds of Prey* (Baltimore, MD, 1995), pp. 30–32.
8 Lerner and Mindell, 'Phylogeny of Eagles', p. 343.
9 Jeff Watson, *The Golden Eagle* (London, 1997), pp. 16–17.
10 Penny Olsen, *Wedge-tailed Eagle* (Collingwood, Victoria, 2005), pp. 16 and 52.
11 Sankar Chatterjee, *The Rise of Birds: 225 Million Years of Evolution* (Baltimore, MD, 1997), pp. 276–81.
12 Scott Weidensaul, *Raptors: The Birds of Prey* (New York, 1996), p. 207.
13 Watson, *Golden Eagle*, pp. 20–31.

14 Josep del Hoyo, *Handbook of the Birds of the World*, II (Barcelona, 1994), p. 56.

15 Bruce E. Beans, *Eagle's Plume: Preserving the Life and Habitat of America's Bald Eagle* (New York, 1996), p. 51.

16 Hoyo, *Handbook of the Birds of the World*, p. 56.

17 Olsen, *Wedge-tailed Eagle*, p. 29.

18 Ibid., p. 32.

19 Leslie Brown, *Birds of Prey: Their Biology and Ecology* (London, 1976), p. 104.

20 Olsen, *Australian Birds of Prey*, p. 20.

21 John Pollard, *Birds in Greek Life and Myth* (London, 1977), p. 14.

22 Arthur Cleveland Bent, *Life Histories of North American Birds of Prey* (New York, 1961), vol. I, p. 331.

23 Beans, *Eagle's Plume*, p. 36.

24 Olsen, *Australian Birds of Prey*, p. 25.

25 Munir Z. Virani, 'African Fish-eagle', in *The Eagle Watchers: Observing and Conserving Raptors around the World*, ed. Ruth E. Tingay and Todd E. Katzner (Ithaca, NY, 2010), p. 155.

26 Weidensaul, *Raptors*, pp. 71–2.

27 Olsen, *Wedge-tailed Eagle*, p. 39.

28 Brown. *Birds of Prey*, pp. 75–6.

29 Brown, *Eagles*, p. 42.

30 Olsen, *Australian Birds of Prey*, p. 100.

31 David M. Bird, *The Bird Almanac: The Ultimate Guide to Essential Facts and Figures of the World's Birds* (Buffalo, NY, 1999), p. 282.

32 Jason Wiersma, 'White-bellied Sea Eagle', in *Eagle Watchers*, ed. Tingay and Katzner, p. 174.

33 Brown, *Eagles*, pp. 52–3.

34 Malcolm Nicoll, 'Grey-headed Fishing Eagle, Cambodia', in *Eagle Watchers*, ed. Tingay and Katzner, p. 126.

35 Brown, *Birds of Prey*, pp. 112–13.

36 Ibid., p. 121.

37 Olsen, *Australian Birds of Prey*, p. 96.

38 Bent, *North American Birds of Prey*, p. 343; Wiedensaul, *Raptors*, p. 169.

39 Mark Hume, 'Starving Eagles "Falling Out of the Sky"',
    Globe and Mail, 23 February 2011.

40 Brown, *Eagles*, p. 47.

41 Weidensaul, *Raptors*, pp. 82–3.

42 Brown, *Eagles*, p. 38.

43 Olsen, *Wedge-tailed Eagle*, pp. 35–6.

44 Björn Helander, 'White-tailed Sea Eagle', in *Eagle Watchers*,
    ed. Tingay and Katzner, p. 198.

45 Ruth Tingay, 'Madagascar Fish Eagle, Madagascar', in *Eagle
    Watchers*, ed. Tingay and Katzner, p. 112.

46 Brown, *Eagles*, pp. 66–8.

47 Olsen, *Australian Birds of Prey*, p. 137.

48 Beans, *Eagle's Plume*, p. 44.

49 Weidensaul, *Raptors*, p. 128.

50 Bridget Stutchbury, *The Private Lives of Birds: A Scientist Reveals the
    Intricacies of Avian Social Life* (New York, 2010), pp. 116–18.

51 Brown, *Eagles*, p. 82.

52 Robert E. Simmons, 'Wahlberg's Eagle, South Africa', in *Eagle
    Watchers*, ed. Tingay and Katzner, p. 137.

53 Beans, *Eagle's Plume*, p. 48.

54 Weidensaul, *Raptors*, pp. 139–50.

55 PostMedia News, 'In Death, Bird a Symbol of Life',
    Times and Transcript (Moncton), 10 November 2010.

56 Brown, *Eagles*, pp. 32–3.

57 Keisuke Saito, 'Steller's Sea Eagle, Japan', in *Eagle Watchers*,
    ed. Tingay and Katzner, pp. 101–4.

58 Helander, 'White-tailed Sea Eagle', p. 199.

59 Susanne Shultz, 'African Crowned Eagle, Ivory Coast', in *Eagle
    Watchers*, ed. Tingay and Katzner, p. 121.

60 John A. Love, 'White-tailed Sea Eagle', in *Eagle Watchers*,
    ed. Tingay and Katzner, p. 205.

61 Weidensaul, *Raptors*, pp. 95–7.

62 Keith L. Bildstein, *Migrating Raptors of the World: Their Ecology and
    Conservation* (Ithaca, NY, and London, 2006), p. 9.

63 Ibid., p. 169.

64 Ibid., pp. 7–14.
65 Ibid., pp. 61–6.

2 SACRED EAGLE: MYTHOLOGY, RELIGION AND FOLKLORE

 1 Jeremy Mynott, *Birdscapes: Birds in Our Imagination and Experience* (Princeton, NJ, 2009), p. 267. This is a rephrasing of Lévi-Strauss's question.
 2 Scott Weidensaul, *Raptors: The Birds of Prey* (New York, 1996), p. 292.
 3 Edward A. Armstrong, *The Folklore of Birds* (New York, 1970), p. 129.
 4 Rudolf Wittkower, 'Eagle and Serpent: A Study in the Migration of Symbols', *Journal of the Warburg Institute*, II (1939), p. 308.
 5 Cassandra Eason, *Fabulous Creatures, Mythical Monsters and Animal Power Symbols: A Handbook* (Westport, CT, 2008), p. 58.
 6 Hartley Burr Alexander, *The Mythology of All Races*, XI: *Latin-American* (New York, 1964), p. 122.
 7 A. F. Scholfield, trans., *Aelian: On the Characteristics of Animals*, III (Cambridge, MA, 1958), p. 127.
 8 J.M.C. Toynbee, *Animals in Roman Life and Art* (Baltimore, MD, 1996), p. 241.
 9 Armstrong, *Folklore of Birds*, p. 133.
10 Weidensaul, *Raptors*, p. 287.
11 Lindsay Jones et al., *Encyclopedia of Religion*, IX (Detroit, MI, 2005), p. 2554.
12 Homer, *Odyssey*, trans. Stanley Lombardo (Indianapolis, IN, 2000), p. 19.
13 The eagle is sometimes portrayed as a vulture: raptor confusion/conflation is common in myth and folklore. There is a similar story in Georgian mythology with a character called Amirani, who also is tortured by an eagle.
14 Virgil, *Aeneid*, trans. Stanley Lombardo (Indianapolis, IN, 2005), p. 109.
15 Ovid, *Metamorphoses*, trans. A. D. Melville (Oxford, 1986), pp. 229–30.

16 John Pollard, *Birds in Greek Life and Myth* (London, 1977), p. 141.

17 Armstrong, *Folklore of Birds*, p. 133.

18 Jones, *Encyclopaedia of Religion*, p. 2553.

19 Pollard, *Birds in Greek Life*, p. 189.

20 Cited in Jean Chevalier and Alain Gheerbrant, *A Dictionary of Symbols*, trans. John Buchanan-Brown (Oxford, 1994), p. 323.

21 John Trevisa, trans., *On the Properties of Things: John Trevisa's Translation of Bartholomeus Anglicus De Proprietatibus Rerum*, I (Oxford, 1975), p. 603.

22 John M. Steadman, 'Chaucer's Eagle: A Contemplative Symbol', *Publications of the Modern Language Association of America*, LXXV (1960), pp. 153–9.

23 Stillman Drake, trans., *Discoveries and Opinions of Galileo* (New York, 1957), p. 239.

24 The medieval commentator Berchorius connected the imagery of the eagle to St John: 'the subtlety and clarity of intellect . . . enabled John the Evangelist to speak of heavenly matters'. Steadman, 'Chaucer's Eagle', p. 157.

25 Georges Dumézil, *Archaic Roman Religion* (Chicago, IL, 1966), vol. II, p. 598.

26 Sarah Iles Johnston, *Ancient Greek Divination* (Chichester, 2008), p. 129.

27 Scholfield, *Aelian: On the Characteristics of Animals*, vol. III, p. 79.

28 Homer, *Odyssey*, trans. Lombardo, p. 20.

29 Scholfield, *Aelian: On the Characteristics of Animals*, I, p. 55.

30 H. Rackham, trans., *Pliny: Natural History* (Cambridge, MA, 1947), vol. III, p. 301.

31 Jacqueline Simpson and Steve Roud, *A Dictionary of English Folklore* (Oxford, 2000), p. 102.

32 Scholfield, *Aelian: On the Characteristics of Animals*, I, p. 63.

33 Uno Holmberg, *The Mythology of All Races*, IV: *Finno-Ugric, Siberian* (New York, 1964), p. 505.

34 A. Berriedale Keith and Albert J. Carnoy, *The Mythology of All Races*, VI: *Indian, Iranian* (New York, 1964), p. 47.

35 Chevalier and Gheerbrant, *Dictionary of Symbols*, p. 327.

36 Sam D. Gill and Irene F. Sullivan, *Dictionary of Native American Mythology* (New York, 1994), p. 37.

37 Armstrong, *Folklore of Birds*, p. 126.

38 Rackham, *Pliny: Natural History*, III, p. 303.

39 Holmberg, *Mythology of All Races*, IV, p. 357.

40 Armstrong, *Folklore of Birds*, p. 140.

41 Drake Stutesman, *Snake* (London, 2005), pp. 33–93.

42 Axel Olrik, *The Mythology of All Races*, II: *Teutonic* (New York, 1964), pp. 179 and 193.

43 John A. MacCulloch and Jan Máchal, *The Mythology of All Races*, III: *Celtic, Slavic* (New York, 1964), p. 97.

44 Nili Wazana, 'Anzu and Ziz: Great Mythical Birds and Ancient Near East, Biblical, and Rabbinic Traditions', *Journal of the Ancient Near East Society*, XXXI (2009), pp. 111–35.

45 Gwendolyn Leick, *A Dictionary of Ancient Near Eastern Mythology* (London, 1991), p. 112.

46 Stephanie Dalley, trans., *Myths of Mesopotamia: Creation, the Flood, Gilgamesh and Others* (Oxford, 1989), pp. 204–27. Thorkild Jacobsen, *The Treasures of Darkness: A History of Mesopotamian Religion* (New Haven, CT, and London, 1976), p. 7.

47 Jones et al., *Encyclopaedia of Religion*, IX, p. 2553.

48 Jacobsen, *Treasures of Darkness*, p. 128.

49 Richard Barber, trans., *Bestiary: Being an English Version of Bodleian Library MS Bodley 764* (Woodbridge, 1992), p. 119.

50 Ibid.

51 All biblical references are taken from *The Holy Bible: Revised Standard Version* (New York, 1952).

52 Wazana, 'Anzu and Ziz: Great Mythical Birds', pp. 129–34.

53 Armstrong, *Folklore of Birds*, p. 129.

54 John Barton and John Muddiman, eds, *The Oxford Bible Commentary* (Oxford, 2001), pp. 538, 1293.

55 Ibid., pp. 775–87.

56 Isaiah 40:31. See also Psalms 23:5.

57 Deuteronomy 32:11. See also Exodus 19:4.

58 Leviticus 11:13. See also Deuteronomy 14:12.

59 2 Samuel 1:23. See also Job 9:26 and Habakkuk 1:8.

60 Mary Ellen Miller, *The Art of Mesoamerica from Olmec to Aztec* (London, 2006), pp. 198 and 221.

61 Elizabeth H. Boone, *Incarnations of the Aztec Supernatural: The Image of Huitzilopochtli in Mexico and Europe* (Philadelphia, PA, 1989), p. 10; Arthur J. O. Anderson and Charles Dibble, trans., *The Florentine Codex*, Bernardino de Sahagún, II (Santa Fe, NM, 1950), pp. 47–8.

62 Boone, *Incarnations of the Aztec Supernatural*, pp. 1–2.

63 Miller, *Art of Mesoamerica*, p. 233.

64 Bill McLennan and Karen Duffek, *The Transforming Image: Painted Arts of Northwest Coast First Nations* (Vancouver, BC, 2000), p. 126.

65 Johanna M. Blows, *Eagle and Crow: An Exploration of an Australian Aboriginal Myth* (New York, 1995), pp. 3–4.

66 'The Story of Flinders Ranges', told by Mincham, cited in Blows, *Eagle and Crow*, p. 32.

67 'Eagle Takes Water to the Sky', Wongaibon people, in Blows, *Eagle and Crow*, p. 86.

68 'The Birth of Eagle', told by Fred Biggs, cited in Blows, *Eagle and Crow*, p. 185.

69 Paul S. C. Tacon, 'The World of Ancient Ancestors: Australian Aboriginal Caves and Other Realms within Rock', *Expedition*, XLVII (2005), pp. 37–47.

70 Eason, *Fabulous Creatures*, p. 83.

71 Aelian saw the relationship between humans and gryphons as adversarial, since humans would try to steal the gryphons' gold-hoard. Scholfield, *Aelian: On the Characteristics of Animals*, I, pp. 27–9.

72 Jones et al., *Encyclopaedia of Religion*, IX, p. 2553.

3 PATRIOTIC EAGLE: FLAGS, HERALDRY AND EMBLEMS

1 Biren Bonnerjea, *A Dictionary of Superstitions and Mythology* (London, 1927), p. 84.

2 A. F. Scholfield, trans., *Aelian: On the Characteristics of Animals*, III (Cambridge, MA, 1958), pp. 39–41.

3 Ibid., p. 41.

4 Manfred Lurker, *Dictionary of Gods and Goddesses, Devils and Demons* (London, 1987), p. 107.

5 H. Rackham, trans., *Pliny: Natural History*, III (Cambridge, MA, 1947), p. 303.

6 Whitney Smith, *Flags through the Ages and Across the World* (New York, 1975), pp. 37–8.

7 Arthur Charles Fox-Davies, *The Art of Heraldry: An Encyclopaedia of Armory* (New York, 1968), p. 170.

8 Leslie Brown, *Birds of Prey: Their Biology and Ecology* (London, 1976), p. 156.

9 Thomas Woodcock and John Martin Robinson, *The Oxford Guide to Heraldry* (Oxford, 1990), p. 199.

10 Bradford B. Broughton, *Dictionary of Medieval Knighthood and Chivalry* (New York, 1996), p. 176.

11 Jennifer Westwood and Jacqueline Simpson, *The Lore of the Land* (London, 2005), pp. 400–401.

12 Lurker, *Dictionary of Gods and Goddesses*, p. 304.

13 For example, Austria, Russia, Serbia and Liechtenstein.

14 Smith, *Flags through the Ages*, pp. 242 and 261.

15 This includes the air forces of Britain, the United States, Canada, Australia, New Zealand, Nigeria and India.

16 Smith, *Flags through the Ages*, pp. 114–15.

17 Eric Michaud, *The Cult of Art in Nazi Germany*, trans. Janet Lloyd (Stanford, CA, 2004), p. 89–115.

18 Robert Jan Van Pelt, 'Bearers of Culture, Harbingers of Destruction: The *Mythos* of Germans in the East', in *Art, Culture and Media under the Third Reich*, ed. Richard A. Etlin (Chicago, IL, 2002), p. 104.

19 Mohawks of the Bay of Quinte, www.mbq-tmt.org, accessed 9 December 2013.

20 Bruce E. Beans, *Eagle's Plume: Preserving the Life and Habitat of America's Bald Eagle* (New York, 1996), p. 58.

21 Ibid., pp. 58–68.

22 Cited in ibid., p. 62.

23 John James Audubon, *Writings and Drawings* (New York, 1999), p. 247.

24 Beans, *Eagle's Plume*, p. 68.

25 Arthur Cleveland Bent, *Life Histories of North American Birds of Prey* (New York, 1961), pt 1, p. 321.

26 Cited in Beans, *Eagle's Plume*, p. 65.

27 Richard H. Zeitlin, *Old Abe the War Eagle* (Madison, WI, 1986).

28 Beans, *Eagle's Plume*, p. 55.

29 Nathaniel Hawthorne, 'The Custom-House', *The Scarlet Letter and Other Writings* (New York, 2005), pp. 8–9.

30 Vincent Nijman, 'Javan Hawk-Eagle', *The Eagle Watchers: Observing and Conserving Raptors around the World*, ed. Ruth E. Tingay and Todd E. Katzner (Ithaca, NY, 2010), pp. 146–52.

4 AESTHETIC EAGLE: ART, LITERATURE AND POPULAR CULTURE

1 'The Blessed Gift of Joy is Bestowed Upon Man', told by Saglaug, in Knut Rasmussen, *The Eagle's Gift: Alaskan Eskimo Tales*, trans. Isobel Hutchinson (New York, 1932), pp. 9–16.

2 Walt Whitman, 'The Dalliance of the Eagles', *Leaves of Grass: Comprehensive Reader's Edition* (New York, 1965), pp. 273–4.

3 Alfred Tennyson, 'The Eagle', *The Poems of Tennyson*, III (Berkeley, CA, 1987), p. 537.

4 A. F. Scholfield, trans., *Aelian: On the Characteristics of Animals*, 3 vols (Cambridge, MA, 1958). Aelian's references to eagles are found in the following books and verses: 1.35; 1.42; 2.26; 3.39; 5.48; 6.29; 6.46; 7.11; 7.16; 7.45; 9.2; 9.10; 12.21.

5 Ibid., II, p. 223.

6 Ibid., II, p. 231.

7 Ibid., II, pp. 47–9.

8 Ibid., II, p. 125.

9 Olivia Temple and Robert Temple, trans., *Aesop: The Complete Fables* (London, 1998), pp. 2–7, 18, 64 and 351.

10 Ibid., p. 7.
11 Cited in John Pollard, *Birds in Greek Life and Myth* (London, 1977), p. 123.
12 Edmund Waller, 'To a Lady Singing a Song of His Composing', *Poetical Works of Edmund Waller* (London, 1854), p. 143.
13 Richard Lattimore, trans., *The Iliad of Homer* (Chicago, IL, 1951), p. 483.
14 Homer, *Odyssey*, trans. Stanley Lombardo (Indianapolis, IN, 2000), p. 20.
15 Ibid., p. 307.
16 Franz Kafka, 'Prometheus', *The Basic Kafka* (New York, 1979), p. 152.
17 Charles W. Kennedy, trans., 'The Battle of Maldon', *An Anthology of Old English Poetry* (New York, 1960), p. 163.
18 Seamus Heaney, trans., *Beowulf: A New Verse Translation* (New York, 2000), p. 203.
19 Ezra Pound, trans., 'The Seafarer', *The Norton Anthology of Poetry*, ed. Margaret Ferguson et al. (New York, 2005), p. 13.
20 Godfrid Storms, *Anglo-Saxon Magic* (The Hague, 1948), p. 155.
21 Roberta Frank, 'Viking Atrocity and Skaldic Verse: The Rite of the Blood-eagle', *English Historical Review*, XCIX (1984), pp. 332–43.
22 Dante, *The Divine Comedy*, II: *Purgatory*, trans. Dorothy L. Sayers (Harmondsworth, 1955), pp. 134–5.
23 Dante, *The Divine Comedy*, III: *Paradise*, trans. Dorothy L. Sayers and Barbara Reynolds (Harmondsworth, 1962), pp. 214–40.
24 Geoffrey Chaucer, 'The House of Fame', *The Riverside Chaucer*, ed. Larry D. Benson (Oxford, 1987), pp. 354–5.
25 Edward A. Armstrong, *Folklore of Birds* (New York, 1970), pp. 135–9.
26 Geoffrey Chaucer, 'The Parliament of Fowls', *The Riverside Chaucer*, ed. Larry D. Benson (Oxford, 1987), pp. 385–94.
27 Larry D. Benson, Introduction, ibid., p. 384.
28 Edmund Spenser, *The Faerie Queene*, The Norton Anthology of English Literature, ed. M. H. Abrams (New York, 2000), I, pp. 757–8.

29 Percy Bysshe Shelley, *The Poetical Works of Percy Bysshe Shelley* (London, 1882), p. 112.

30 William Blake, *The Complete Poetry and Prose of William Blake* (Berkeley, CA, 2008), p. 37.

31 Morris Eaves, ed., *The Cambridge Companion to William Blake* (Cambridge, 2003), p. 48; Blake, *Complete Poetry and Prose*, p. 40.

32 Ibid., p. 37.

33 Ibid., p. 3.

34 T. S. Eliot, *The Rock* (New York, 1934), p. 7.

35 Alfred Tennyson, 'The Eagle', *The Poems of Tennyson*, II (Berkeley, CA, 1987), p. 444.

36 Martin Kemp, *The Human Animal in Western Art and Science* (Chicago, IL, 2007), p. 97.

37 Ibid., p. 116.

38 Hugo Munsterberg, *Dictionary of Chinese and Japanese Art* (New York, 1981), p. 15.

39 Pacific Asia Museum, 'Nature of the Beast: Animals in Japanese Paintings and Prints', www.pacificasiamuseum.org, accessed 10 December 2013.

40 Ralph Croizier, *Art and Revolution in Modern China: The Lingnan (Cantonese) School of Painting, 1909–1951* (Berkeley, CA, 1988), p. 89.

41 Katherine M. Ball, *Animal Motifs in Asian Art: An Illustrated Guide to their Meanings and Aesthetics* (New York, 2004), p. 215.

42 Harold P. Stern, *Birds, Beasts, Blossoms and Bugs: The Nature of Japan* (New York, 1976), p. 104.

43 E. B. White, 'The Deserted Nation', *The New Yorker* (8 October 1966), p. 53.

44 Laurence Ferlinghetti, 'I am Waiting', *A Coney Island of the Mind* (New York, 1958), p. 51.

45 Elinor Wylie, *Collected Poems of Elinor Wylie* (New York, 1933), p. 4.

46 Carl Sandburg, 'Wilderness', *Complete Poems* (New York, 1950), p. 100.

47 Joy Harjo, *In Mad Love and War* (Hanover, NH, 1990), p. 65.

48 Robert Francis, 'Eagle Plain', *Collected Poems, 1936–1976* (Amherst, MA, 1976), p. 209.

49 For a description of The Eagle Rock Rock and Eagle Shop, see
   www.hubbyco.com, accessed 10 December 2013.

50 'An Eagle Myth about Flying Swallows and a Wolf Dance in
   a Clay Bank', told by Arnasungak, in Rasmussen, *The Eagle's Gift*,
   pp. 32–3.

5 EAGLES IN OUR WORLD

1 Scott Weidensaul, *Raptors: Birds of Prey* (New York, 1996), p. 295.

2 Jeff Watson, *The Golden Eagle* (London, 1997), p. 260.

3 Ibid., p. 260.

4 Bruce E. Beans, *Eagle's Plume: Preserving the Life and Habitat
   of America's Bald Eagle* (New York, 1996), p. 262.

5 Leslie Brown, *Eagles* (New York and London, 1970), p. 90.

6 Penny Olsen, *Wedge-tailed Eagle* (Collingwood, Melbourne, 2005),
   pp. 8–9.

7 Stephen J. Bodio, *Eagle Dreams: Searching for Legends in Wild
   Mongolia* (Guilford, CT, 2003), p. 146.

8 A. C. Bent, *Life Histories of North American Birds of Prey*
   (New York, 1961), pt 1, p. 331.

9 Watson, *Golden Eagle*, p. 264.

10 Bill Bryson, *At Home: A Short History of Private Life*
   (New York, 2010), p. 52.

11 Penny Olsen, *Australian Birds of Prey: The Biology and Ecology of
   Raptors* (Baltimore, MD, 1995), p. 81.

12 Cited in Beans, *Eagle's Plume*, p. 82

13 Ibid., pp. 77 and 81; Weidensaul, *Raptors*, pp. 221–3.

14 Penny Olsen, 'Wedge-tailed Eagle, Australia', in *The Eagle
   Watchers: Observing and Conserving Raptors around the World*,
   ed. Ruth E. Tingay and Todd E. Katzner (Ithaca, NY, 2010), p. 62.

15 Olsen, *Wedge-tailed Eagle*, p. 85.

16 Watson, *Golden Eagle*, pp. 70–71; Olsen, *Wedge-tailed Eagle*, p. 80.

17 Watson, *Golden Eagle*, p. 72.

18 Beans, *Eagle's Plume*, p. 215.

19 Bent, *North American Birds of Prey*, p. 311.

20 William Holmes McGuffey, *McGuffey's New Sixth Eclectic Reader* (Cincinnati, OH, 1857), pp. 277–83.

21 Susanne Shultz, 'African Crowned Eagle, Ivory Coast', in *Eagle Watchers*, ed. Tingay and Katzner, p. 119.

22 W. Scott McGraw, Catherine Cooke and Susanne Shultz, 'Primate Remains from African Crowned Eagle (*Stephanoaetus coronatu*s) Nests in Ivory Coast's Tai Forest: Implications for Primate Predation and Early Hominid Taphonomy in South Africa', *American Journal of Physical Anthropology*, CXXXI (2006), pp. 151–65.

23 R. Paul Scofield and Ken W. S. Ashwell, 'Rapid Somatic Expansion Causes the Brain to Lag Behind: The Case of the Brain and Behavior of New Zealand's Haast's Eagle (*Harpagornis moorei*)', *Journal of Vertebrate Paleontology*, XXIX (2009), p. 648.

24 Keisuke Saito, 'Steller's Sea Eagle, Japan,' in *Eagle Watchers*, ed. Tingay and Katzner, pp. 101–4.

25 Olsen, *Australian Birds of Prey*, p. 181.

26 Beans, *Eagle's Plume*, p. 245.

27 Olsen, *Wedge-tailed Eagle*, p. 88.

28 Weidensaul, *Raptors*, p. 216.

29 Miguel Ferrer, 'Spanish Imperial Eagle, Spain', in *Eagle Watchers*, ed. Tingay and Katzner, pp. 106–8.

30 'Spanish Imperial Eagle', BirdLife International, www.birdlife.org, accessed 11 December 2013.

31 Kathryn Burnham, 'Eaglet Freed in Dramatic Live-broadcast from Victoria, BC', *Calgary Herald*, 20 May 2011.

32 Penny Olsen, 'Wedge-tailed Eagle, Australia', in *Eagle Watchers*, ed. Tingay and Katzner, p. 64.

Select Bibliography

Armstrong, Edward A., *The Folklore of Birds* (New York, 1970)

Beans, Bruce E., *Eagle's Plume: Preserving the Life and Habitat of America's Bald Eagle* (New York, 1996)

Bent, Arthur Cleveland, *Life Histories of North American Birds of Prey* (New York, 1961)

Blows, Johanna M., *Eagle and Crow: An Exploration of an Australian Aboriginal Myth* (New York, 1995)

Bodio, Stephen J., *Eagle Dreams: Searching for Legends in Wild Mongolia* (Guilford, CT, 2003).

Brown, Leslie, *Birds of Prey: Their Biology and Ecology* (London, 1976)

——, *Eagles* (New York and London, 1970)

Lerner, Heather, and David P. Mindell, 'Phylogeny of Eagles, Old World Vultures and Other Accipitridae Based on Nuclear and Mitochondrial DNA', *Molecular Phylogenetics and Evolution*, XXXVII (2005), pp. 327–46

Mynott, Jeremy, *Birdscapes: Birds in our Imagination and Experience* (Princeton, NJ, 2009)

Olsen, Penny, *Wedge-tailed Eagle* (Collingwood, Melbourne, 2005)

——, *Australian Birds of Prey* (Baltimore, MD, 1995)

Pollard, John, *Birds in Greek Life and Myth* (London, 1977)

Tingay, Ruth E., and Todd E. Katzner, eds, *The Eagle Watchers: Observing and Conserving Raptors around the World* (Ithaca, NY, 2010)

Watson, Jeff, *The Golden Eagle* (London, 1997)

Weidensaul, Scott, *Raptors: The Birds of Prey* (New York, 1996)

Associations and Websites

EUROPEAN RAPTORS
http://europeanraptors.org

BIRDS OF PREY FOUNDATION
www.birds-of-prey.org

RAPTOR RESOURCE PROJECT
www.raptorresource.org

THE RAPTOR FOUNDATION
www.raptorfoundation.org.uk

GLOBAL RAPTOR EDUCATION NETWORK (THE PEREGRINE FUND)
www.globalraptors.org

THE GOLDEN EAGLE TRUST
www.goldeneagle.ie

WEDGE-TAILED EAGLE SITE
www.wedgetaileagle.org.au

U.S. FISH AND WILDLIFE SERVICE, MIDWEST REGION
bald eagle information www.fws.gov/midwest/eagle

Acknowledgements

Thanks to ornithologist Gay Hansen for all her help and enthusiasm, and to Jonathan Burt, Charlotte Sleigh, Alan Rauch, Michael Leaman and the staff at Reaktion. Special thanks to the fabulous Foy sisters, Lea and Sidney, for text and image management. Deepest appreciation to Julia Fleur McMillan for shepherding the manuscript through the final stages of publication.

Photo Acknowledgements

The author and the publishers wish to express their thanks to the below sources of illustrative material and /or permission to reproduce it.

© The Trustees of the British Museum, London: pp. 60, 69, 79, 81, 89, 131, 32; Bibliothèque Nationale de France: p. 54; Buffalo Bill Historical Center: p. 74; Bundesarchiv, Bild 101III-Wisniewski-001-17 / Wisniewski / German Federal Archives: p. 95; Kevin Burkett: p. 137; Al Chapman: p. 37; Jean Charlot: p. 62; Bohus Cicel: p. 9; COA Public Domain by German Gov: p. 94; Jitze Couperus / Flickr Harpy Eagle II: p. 19; DickDaniels (http://carolinabirds.org); Artist Robert Davidson / Photo Joe Mabel: p. 75; Executive Office of the President of the United States: p. 99; Ramon Fvelasquez: p. 18; Michael Gäbler: p. 27; Hermitage Museum, St Petersburg: p. 113; John Carter Brown Library / Archive of Early American Images / World Digital Library: p. 71; Johnson Space Center of the United States National Aeronautics and Space Administration: p. 139; Yathin S. Krishnappa: p. 13; Library of Congress, Washington, DC: pp. 39, 96, 98, 101, 106, 133; Louvre Museum: p. 78; Louvre Museum / Department of Greek, Etruscan and Roman Antiquities / Campana Collection 1861: p. 115 top; Eduardo Merille / Flickr: p. 149; © Ad Meskens / Archeological Museum of Sousse: p. 52; Musée National du Moyen Âge: p. 67; Nez Perce National Historical Park: p. 144 bottom; James Niland / Flickr Nom nom: p. 160; Carsten-Norgaard: p. 115 bottom; One Feather Photos: p. 58 (Scott McKie B.P.); Philadelphia Museum of Art: p. 119; Guillaume Piolle: p. 83; Public Library of Science: p. 23 (John Megahan); Carole Raddato: p. 85; Red

Index